YEAR C

AFTER PENTECOST 2

YEAR C
AFTER PENTECOST 2

PREACHING
THE REVISED
COMMON
LECTIONARY

Marion Soards
Thomas Dozeman
Kendall McCabe

ABINGDON PRESS
Nashville

PREACHING THE REVISED COMMON LECTIONARY
YEAR C: AFTER PENTECOST 2

Copyright © 1994 by Abingdon Press

This book is printed on recycled, acid-free paper.

Library of Congress Cataloging-in-Publication Data
(Revised for vol. 4)

Soards, Marion L., 1952–
    Preaching the Revised common lectionary : year C.

    Includes indexes.
    Contents: [1] Advent/Christmas/Epiphany.—
    [2] Lent/Easter — [3] After Pentecost I. — [4] After Pentecost 2.
        1. Lectionary preaching. 2. Bible—Homiletical use. I. Dozeman, Thomas B.
    II. McCabe, Kendall, 1939–   . III. Title.   IV. Title: Common lectionary (1992)
        BV4235.L43S63   1994   251   93-30550
    ISBN 0-687-33804-2 (v. 1 : alk paper)
    ISBN 0-687-33805-0 (v. 2 : alk paper)
    ISBN 0-687-33806-9 (v. 3 : alk paper)
    ISBN 0-687-33807-7 (v. 4 : alk paper)

Scripture quotations, unless otherwise noted, are from the New Revised Standard Version of the Bible, copyright © 1989 by the Division of Christian Education of the National Council of the Churches of Christ in the USA. Used by permission.

Scripture quotations marked AP are the author's paraphrase of the Bible.

94 95 96 97 98 99 00 01 02 03 — 10 9 8 7 6 5 4 3 2 1

MANUFACTURED IN THE UNITED STATES OF AMERICA

Contents

CONTENTS

This is one volume in a twelve-volume series. Each volume contains commentary and worship suggestions for a portion of the lectionary cycle A, B, or C. Since the lections for a few special days do not change from one lectionary cycle to another, material for each of these days appears in only one of the volumes. Appropriate cross references in the table of contents lead the reader to material in other volumes of the series.

Introduction

Now pastors and students have a systematic treatment of essential issues of the Christian year and Bible study for worship and proclamation based on the Revised Common Lectionary. Interpretation of the lectionary will separate into three parts: Calendar, Canon, and Celebration. A brief word of introduction will provide helpful guidelines for utilizing this resource in worship through the Christian year.

Calendar. Every season of the Christian year will be introduced with a theological interpretation of its meaning, and how it relates to the overall Christian year. This section will also include specific liturgical suggestions for the season.

Canon. The lectionary passages will be interpreted in terms of their setting, structure, and significance. First, the word *setting* is being used loosely in this commentary to include a range of different contexts in which biblical texts can be interpreted from literary setting to historical or cultic settings. Second, regardless of how the text is approached under the heading of setting, interpretation will always proceed to an analysis of the structure of the text under study. Third, under the heading of significance, central themes and motifs of the passage will be underscored to provide a theological interpretation of the text as a springboard for preaching. Thus interpretation of the lectionary passages will result in the outline on the next page.

Celebration. This section will focus on specific ways of relating the lessons to liturgical acts and/or homiletical options for the day on which they occur. How the texts have been used in the Christian tradition will sometimes be illustrated to stimulate the thinking of preachers and planners of worship services.

I. OLD TESTAMENT TEXTS

A. The Old Testament Lesson

1. Setting

2. Structure

3. Significance

B. Psalm

1. Setting

2. Structure

3. Significance

II. NEW TESTAMENT TEXTS

A. The Epistle

1. Setting

2. Structure

3. Significance

B. The Gospel

1. Setting

2. Structure

3. Significance

Why We Use the Lectionary

Although many denominations have been officially or unofficially using some form of the lectionary for many years, some pastors are still unclear about where it comes from, why some lectionaries differ from denomination to denomination, and why the use of a lectionary is to be preferred to a more random sampling of scripture.

Simply put, the use of a lectionary provides a more diverse scriptural diet for God's people, and it can help protect the congregation from the whims and prejudices of the pastor and other worship planners. Faithful use of the lectionary means that preachers must deal with texts they had rather ignore, but about which the congregation may have great concern and interest. The story of the dishonest servant, which we encounter in this volume at Proper 20, might be a case in point. Adherence to the lectionary can be an antidote to that homiletical arrogance that says, "I know what my people need," and in humility acknowledges that the Word of God found in scripture may speak to more needs on Sunday morning than we even know exist, when we seek to proclaim faithfully the message we have wrestled from the text.

The lectionary may also serve as a resource for liturgical content. The psalm is intended to be a response to the Old Testament lesson, and not read as a lesson itself, but beyond that the lessons may inform the content of prayers of confession, intercession, and petition. Some lessons may be adapted as affirmations of faith, as in *The United Methodist Hymnal,* nos. 887-89; the United Church of Christ's *Hymnal,* nos. 429-30; and the Presbyterian *Worshipbook,* no. 30. The "Celebration" entries for each day will call attention to these opportunities from time to time.

Pastors and preachers in the free-church tradition should think of the lectionary as a primary resource for preaching and worship, but need to remember that the lectionary was made for them and not they for the lectionary. The lectionary may serve as the inspiration for a separate series of lessons and sermons that will include texts not in the present edition, or having chosen one of the lectionary passages as the basis for the day's sermon, the preacher may wish to make an independent choice of the other lessons to supplement and illustrate the primary text. The lectionary will be of most value when its use is not a cause for legalism but for inspiration. Pastors who experience a love/hate relationship with the lectionary will gain much sympathy and guidance from Eugene Lowry's penetrating analysis in *Living with the Lectionary: Preaching Through the Revised Common Lectionary* (Nashville: Abingdon Press, 1992).

Just as there are no perfect preachers, there are no perfect lectionaries. The Revised Common Lectionary, upon which this series is based, is the result of the work of many years by the Consultation on Common Texts and is a response to ongoing evaluation of the Common Lectionary (1983) by pastors and scholars from the several participating denominations. The current interest in the lectionary can be traced back to the Second Vatican Council, which ordered lectionary revision for the Roman Catholic Church:

> The treasures of the Bible are to be opened up more lavishly, so that richer fare may be provided for the faithful at the table of God's Word. In this way a more representative portion of the holy Scriptures will be read to the people over a set cycle of years. (*The Documents of Vatican II,* Walter Abbott, ed. [Piscataway, N.J.: New Century, 1974], p. 155)

The example thus set by Roman Catholics inspired Protestants to take more seriously the place of the Bible in their services and sermons, and soon many denominations had issued their own three-year cycles, based generally on the Roman Catholic model, but with their own modifications. This explains why some discrepancies and variations appear in different forms of the lectionary. The Revised Common Lectionary (RCL) is an effort to increase agreement among the churches. A table at the end of the volume will list the differences among the RCL and the Roman Catholic, Episcopal, and Lutheran lectionaries. Where no entry is made, all are in agreement with the RCL.

For those unacquainted with the general pattern of the lectionary, a brief word of explanation may be helpful for sermon preparation.

(1) The three years are each distinguished by one of the Synoptic Gospels: Matthew in A, Mark in B, Luke in C. John is distributed over the three years with a heavy emphasis during Lent and Easter. (2) Two types of readings are used. During the periods of Advent to Epiphany and Lent to Pentecost, the readings are usually topical—that is, there is some common theme among them. During the Sundays after Epiphany and Pentecost the readings are continuous, with no necessary connection between the lessons. In the period covered by this volume, there is a thematic connection between the Old Testament lesson and the Gospel during the Sundays after Epiphany, but the epistle lesson begins a continuous reading from I Corinthians. The preacher begins, then, with at least four preaching options: to deal with either one of the lessons on their own or to work with the dialogue between the Old Testament lesson and the Gospel. Perhaps it should also be added that though the psalm is intended to be a response by the people to the Old Testament lesson—rather than as a lesson on its own—this in no way suggests that it cannot be used as the text for the sermon.

This is the last of four volumes that will deal with the lessons for the entire C Cycle of the Christian year. The first volume covered Advent through the Sundays after Epiphany. The second volume included Ash Wednesday through the Day of Pentecost. The third volume began with Trinity Sunday (the First Sunday After Pentecost) and included all the lessons for June, July, and August. This volume finishes the remainder of the year, including the lessons for All Saints' Day (November 1). Years A and B have been published previously, also in two series of four volumes each.

A note on language: We have used the term *Old Testament* in this series because that is the language employed by the Consultation on Common Texts, at least up to this point. Pastors and worship committees may wish to consider alternative terms, such as *First Testament* or *Hebrew Scriptures,* that do not imply that those writings somehow have less value than the rest of the Christian Bible. Another option is to refer to *First Lesson* (always from the Hebrew Scriptures), *Second Lesson* (from Acts, Revelation, or the epistles), and *Gospel.*

PREACHING AND WORSHIP AMIDST THE CLASH OF CALENDARS

Perhaps at no other time of the year than in the autumn do preachers and planners of worship experience so many demands upon them for attention by diverse programmatic and special interest concerns. Three calendars are usually competing for attention all the year round, with varying degrees of success at different times.

The most important, of course, is the Christian year calendar itself, which guides us through the varied acts in the drama of our salvation with commentary provided by the lectionary all along the way. The observance of that calendar and the lectionary keeps the Church faithful to the Easter proclamation, since the purpose of the Christian year is to assist us in examining the Easter mystery from different perspectives. The regular return of the Lord's Day reminds us that we are an Easter people, a product of the eighth day of creation, and that through baptism we have been born from above and are now engaged upon a pilgrimage in which we are seeking the things that are above.

The Church's programmatic calendar is another significant factor in planning for preaching and worship, particularly in the autumn. For many churches this is the time to swing into action after summer recess. Church school resumes, or if it has not stopped, students now move to different classes. Choirs once more reappear, and it is not unknown for "Back to Church Sunday" to be marked by the donning of vestments or robes that were abandoned after Memorial Day. The denomination as well as the local church uses this time to make special emphases. A kind of pan-Protestant calendar observes annually in the autumn Christian Education Sunday, World Communion Sunday, Laity Sunday, Stewardship Sunday, and National Bible Sunday. Depending upon the particular denomination, one may also be expected to observe Reformation Sunday and United Nations Sunday as well. Homecoming Sunday is regularly observed in autumn by many congregations. Frequently these days come equipped by the denominational program agencies with special orders of service, scripture lessons, even sermon outlines. Without denying the legitimacy and appropriateness of the interests represented, it may still be said that among American Protestants the program Sunday threatens to do to the regular pattern of Christian year and lectionary what the saints days did to the dominical pattern of worship in the medieval church.

The civil calendar is the third contender for the attention of the congregation. In some ways the first of September is the beginning of a new year in the civil calendar. The beginning of school might be said to exercise more influence over the national life than any other single event, so by those dates vacations are planned, houses are bought and sold, clothes are purchased, schedules are arranged. Labor Day weekend is a significant date on many counts, and so it is not unusual to find sermon topics for the Sunday that deal not only with labor but with beginnings. Election Day and Veterans Day do not appeal as much to a pulpit setting, but they have been known to become primary themes for the Lord's Day. Perhaps the most difficult issue to deal with in terms of the civil calendar is that of Thanksgiving, because it is so entwined with our national and religious roots. It is easy to forget that Thanksgiving Day is not a day of the Church (since, eucharistically speaking, for the Church every Sunday is Thanksgiving Day), but is a patriotic occasion dictated by a presidential proclamation. And what the president proclaims is Thanksgiving Day, the fourth Thursday in November, not Thanksgiving Sunday. Yet often a Thanksgiving Sunday is invented so that the people are relieved of the patriotic burden of attending church more than once a week. The Sunday that is thus lost from the Christian year is Christ the King, the very Sunday that allows us to proclaim that we have no time for civil religion and that our citizenship is in heaven! Preachers who wish to explore more fully the implications of the civil calendar for Christian proclamation will find challenging reading in Stanley Hauerwas's *Unleashing the Scripture: Freeing the Bible from Captivity to America* (Nashville: Abingdon, 1993).

Because Christianity is incarnational, designed to relate to the world in which we live, all three calendars need to be taken seriously. The question becomes one of deciding how Christian preaching and worship relate to the three and by what principles we set priorities among them. Certain affirmations need to be made and regulations established in order to avoid both liturgical chaos and a homiletical pattern that is only a response to squeaking wheels in church or society. For persons who exercise gospel freedom, law is important because it gives us an excuse for breaking it!

1. We affirm the priority of the Lord's Day as the day of the Christian assembly, which meets primarily for the purpose of retelling the story and responding to the story in sacramental actions.

2. We affirm the priority of the lectionary as the primary means by which the story is told and remembered in an orderly and coherent fashion.

3. We affirm the relevance of the scriptures to Christian living as a gift of God. The Bible is not something we have to "make relevant" to our lives, or through which we search to find relevant passages; as "Word of God" it addresses the depths of our being as we open ourselves to it in earnest prayer and committed study.

4. We affirm the movement from word and sacrament in the assembly to a life of service in the world as the Church becomes God's word and sacrament for the world. Preaching and liturgy lead us to a participation in the sacrificial life of Christ. Christians then have a responsibility to know about the world and its concerns so that our ministry may be both compassionate and informed.

Adherence to these affirmations can help keep the scriptures at the center of the congregation's worship life without using them in a haphazard fashion to serve some purely thematic end. For example, when confronted with the necessity of preaching on Labor Day weekend, the preacher's pattern should not be to decide what he or she thinks about the labor / management issues of the day and then find some umbrella scripture lesson that might relate in a vague way, but need not be referred to at length. The first Sunday in September will generally have the lessons of Proper Eighteen. In Year C, the Old Testament lesson from Jeremiah, while depicting a setting of human labor, the potter's shed, is of little help in dealing with the subject of our labor and its place in the world. The epistle reading, however, is Paul's letter to Philemon, a letter that will revolutionize Christian thinking about the relation of master and slave. By extension it can speak to our time about proper relationships between employer and employee, relationships that have their origins in a mutual baptism. The Gospel reading (Luke 14:25-33) is a challenge to ask about the end of our labor. How is our everyday work a part of our Christian vocation and our carrying of the cross? It brings us to a re-examination of our presuppostions about what constitutes the "good life" in a society where work is valued only for the possessions it helps us acquire. Surely these lessons can lead the preacher to address whatever issues may be significant locally, nationally, or globally for the ordering of the relationship between labor and management and rich and poor, and the meaning of work in a Christian context.

It must be admitted that the limitations of the lectionary may seem rather obvious for those traditions that celebrate the Eucharist infrequently, but usually on the first Sunday in October, World Communion Sunday. In Year C the preacher is confronted with the opening verses of Lamentations and II Timothy, and with two sayings of Jesus in Luke, one about faith and the other about being worthless slaves ("unprofitable servants" in the KJV) after doing all we have been ordered to do. There appears to be little that is directly applicable to the theme of Christian unity around the Lord's Table. It may be necessary to rid oneself of the impression that the texts (and the sermon) need to deal with the Lord's Supper every time the Lord's Supper is observed. Rather, if the Eucharist is bread for the journey, then it is important to spread the table at the time God's people are confronting head on the tough questions about life and living. The Eucharist is the sign of Christ's continuing, nourishing, supportive presence in the midst of the assembly. When we gather around the dinner table, it is not necessary to discuss the nutritional components of each course for us to benefit from them! In the same way, every aspect of the Lord's Supper need not be cognitively spelled out for individuals and the community to appropriate its power. See the "Celebration" entry for Proper Twenty-two to explore some ways these texts may contribute to a fuller understanding of what it means to discover our unity in the common life God gives around a common table.

The sequential character of the lessons allows for a seasonal series of sermons; only the preacher's imagination can limit how these may be employed. The Old Testament lessons draw primarily from Jeremiah. The epistle lessons can allow for an extended series of expository sermons from the letters to Timothy and II Thessalonians. The Gospel lessons are in most cases accounts of Jesus' teaching ministry and parables about the nature of life in the kingdom. This may provide an opportunity for a sermon series on the characteristics of the Reign of God, culminating in the Gospel reading from Luke's Passion narrative on the Festival of Christ the King.

As a time of new beginnings, this autumn may also be an opportunity for the preacher to make some New Years' resolutions about preaching. Such resolutions may include fixing a time for study and preparation on one's weekly calendar and keeping to it as inflexibly as one does official board meetings, so that sermon preparation is not relegated to the off-times and the residue of the week. Likewise, disciplined prayer time as preparation for preaching needs be worked into the schedule. A daily office should be devised by each working pastor as a means of doing the minimal work of prayer, and it should be adhered to whether one likes it or not, because that is what an office is: *officium,* a duty. There is nothing magical here, but there is something formative for a life in the Spirit that is more than psychological self-help.

The visuals for this long end of the year are green (except for Christ the King and when All Saints is celebrated on the first Sunday in November, and then the color is white or gold). Many churches alter the basic green throughout the autumn to move with the changing color of the leaves, picking up more reds and browns and oranges and yellows. Green should still predominate, however, with its suggestion of life and growth.

Proper Eighteen Sunday Between September 4 and 10 Inclusive

Old Testament Texts

Jeremiah 18:1-11 is the account of the prophet Jeremiah watching a potter work with clay, which then provides analogy to explore God's relationship with humans. Psalm 139 is a hymn of praise to God, from whom no human can flee.

The Lesson: *Jeremiah 18:1-11*

The Potter and the Clay

Setting. Jeremiah 18–19 contain a combination of narratives and poetry that are loosely connected around the image of pottery. Jeremiah 18 begins with the account of Jeremiah in the potter's house (vv. 1-12), which is followed by two poems (a judgment oracle against Israel in vv. 13-17 and a lament by the prophet in vv. 19-23). Jeremiah 19 returns to the motif of pottery when the prophet is commanded to buy an earthen jug, to proclaim judgment on Jerusalem, and then to smash the pot. Jeremiah 19 is clearly a negative message of destruction and doom. The question arises, however, whether the vision of the potter fashioning clay in Jeremiah 18:1-11 is also intended to be a negative message of doom. An answer to this question is the central task required in preaching this text. Is the vision of the potter and the clay a message of hope or doom?

Structure. The lectionary reading stops short of the poetry in Jeremiah 18:13-17, and it has also excluded the narrative in v. 12, choosing to read this as an introduction to an oracle of judgment in vv. 13-17, rather than as a conclusion to the preceding narrative in vv. 1-11. The placement of v. 12 is crucial for interpreting Jeremiah

19

18 as will become clear from an overview of the structure of Jeremiah 18:1-11. The passage separates into three parts. Verses 1-6 recount how Jeremiah received a divine message to observe the work of a potter, especially how clay could be damaged in the process of its formation and then remade. This action provides the occasion for a divine word to the prophet in v. 6: Israel is like clay in God's hands. Verses 7-10 appear to build off the preceding story by providing two instances of how God relates to humans. Note how the syntax emphasizes contrast and how it is repeated in vv. 7-8 and 9-10 ("At one moment . . . but"). The first contrast concerns divine judgment (pluck up, break down, destroy) that is reversed because of human repentance, while the second contrast concerns divine blessing (build and plant) that is reversed because of human evil. Verses 11-12 continue the contrast, but instead of the a-temporal general statements of vv. 7-10, the focus is clearly in the present time and focused on the people of Jerusalem ("Now, therefore, say to the people of Judah and the inhabitants of Jerusalem . . . But they say"). This structure suggests that v. 12 provides a conclusion to the preceding material and that the action of the potter and the clay evolves into a negative story. The question remains, however, whether Jeremiah 18 must necessarily be a negative story.

Significance. Jeremiah 18 is a story about change. The imagery suggests that change is essential both to the divine character and to humans, and, because of this, change is also a central characteristic of the divine-human relationship. Such an emphasis on change introduces ambiguity and unpredictability into the life of faith.

Verses 1-6 can be read as an independent unit. The focus throughout these verses is on God, who is conceived of as a potter. In this reading the potter is at work forming clay, which has its own resiliency in the process of formation. Thus clay is far from a passive substance in pottery, and the result of this is a constant interchange between the fingers of the potter and the properties of the clay. Mistakes are inevitable. Not every pot that is thrown will meet the standards of the potter. The active character of the substance of clay means that skewed shapes do not result in its disposal, but in its being reworked. The oracle to the prophet in vv. 5-6 is a divine self-revelation more than it is a prediction about Israel or their outcome.

The divine self-revelation is that God is a potter. The point about this identification is not to emphasize Israel's passivity over against an all-powerful God who acts on humans objects. Rather the analogy is meant to underscore God's power to stay with the process of formation. Thus, when the focus of the analogy is on God (as is the case in vv. 1-6) the metaphor of the potter and clay is a message of hope, which is meant to proclaim that failed processes can begin again. Just as clay is reworked in the hands of a skillful potter, so Israel can be constantly reshaped by God. Here change is inherent to the divine-human relation, and it is viewed only positively.

Verses 7-10 shift the focus from God to humans in order to explore change from the point of view of clay or humans and how human action influences God. Verses 7-8 explore repentance and its effects on God, while vv. 8-10 reverse the scenario and sketch out sin (conceived of as resistence to change or, to use the words of the text, "not listening to [God's] voice") with its effects on God. Three aspects stand out when these verses are read in conjunction with the opening section. First, the analogy of Israel being clay in the hands of God, the potter, begins to break down when the focus is on humans rather than God, since the clay really becomes the determining factor instead of the potter. Second, humans play a decisive role in determining change within God's character. The image in vv. 7-10 is of God modulating in response to human actions. And third, resistance to change—conceived of as the voice of God—is evil. In summary, change remains the central focus in this section, so much so, in fact, that sin is conceived of as resistance to change.

Verses 11-12 shift the focus once again back to God. Notice how the "I" statements in the divine oracle dominate once again. These verses, however, are not a simple continuation of vv. 1-6. Rather they now take into account the emphasis on the clay that was underscored in vv. 7-10, so that the oracle to contemporary Jerusalem must be read more in light of vv. 7-10 than vv. 1-6. The point of vv. 11-12 is this: When the focus shifts from the potter to the clay, then what had been a message of infinite or unending hope (as in vv. 1-6) is given very specific temporal boundaries ("Now, therefore, . . ."). The focus on the immediate or present moment in v. 12 underscores how human resistance to change—conceived of as God's voice or call to repentance—can short-circuit the unending process of the potter and the clay that was sketched out in vv. 1-6. God may modulate with human action for a time and perhaps even indefinitely as long as the clay is supple, but God does not vascilate indefinitely with resistance. The negative conclusion of the test is that a divine call to repentence (v. 12) is a wake up message that may one day not be repeated.

The Response: *Psalm 139:1-6, 13-18*

A Hymn of Praise

Setting. The description of Psalm 139 in the heading as a hymn of praise is in fact not so clear. There is a didactic or wisdom quality to Psalm 139, in which the psalmist appears to teach those around her about the omnipresence of God, while the end of the psalm actually becomes a lament. The psalm is called a hymn to avoid the danger of reading this litany of divine power and presence as though it were impersonal. The content of the psalm arises out of the experience of the psalmist, which makes the statement about the absolute control of God over all time and space a source of praise. This is not a psalm that explores the dialectic of freedom and necessity.

Structure. The larger structure of Psalm 139 separates into two parts: vv. 1-18 are a hymn and vv. 19-24 are a lament. The mood between these two sections is so sharp that a number of scholars have argued for two separated psalms. This may in fact be the case. The only problem with this conclusion, however, is the close tie between vv. 1 and 23.

The lectionary reading is a portion of the first part of the hymn. Verses 1-18 separate into three parts: vv. 1-6 is a confession of how intimately God knows the psalmist, vv. 7-12 reflect on the omnipresence of God through creation, while vv. 13-18 continue the reflection by moving to the more intimate metaphors of how God was present in the creation of the psalmist.

Significance. The central point of this hymn is in seeing the combination of vv. 7-12 and 13-17. Verses 7-12 underscore how God is everywhere by showing how the psalmist cannot escape the spirit in either heaven or hell (v. 7-8), in the furthermost reaches of the earth

(vv. 9-10), or even through magical incantations of conjuring up darkness (v. 11-12). Such conceptions of omnipresence could be terrifying, but what makes them a springboard of praise is the change in the direction of images from the outer reaches of cosmology in vv. 7-12 to the intimacy of the psalmist's own creation in vv. 13-18. The imagery of God's presence in the privacy of the mother's womb in v. 13 may be anatomical, but it is more likely a reference to the earth. Note how v. 15 continues the imagery of v. 13 and explicitly states that the place of secret formation is the depths of the earth. In either case the point of this imagery is that the omnipresence of God is at the very origin of our creation. God has even beheld our unformed substance (v. 16), hence there is really nothing left to hide. The psalmist concludes from this that God's presence is not something to be avoided or feared but embraced, even when we cannot imagine how, or in what ways, our life's journey interweaves with God (v. 18). Psalm 139 emphasizes the positive message of Jeremiah 18. The constant presence of God with persons of faith (here the psalmist) implies that God stays with processes regardless of their immediate outcome.

New Testament Texts

Philemon presents one of the best opportunities for recognizing the subtlety, charm, wit, and profundity of the apostle Paul. The letter is easily misunderstood and passed over as insignificant, because English translations obscure the wealth of puns and word plays that characterize the Greek text. Jesus' teaching in the Gospel lesson is a set of hard sayings about the costs of discipleship, recognizing the uncompromising nature of the claim laid upon human life by Christ's call.

The Epistle: *Philemon 1-21*

The Formation and Transformation of Relationships in Christ

Setting. Philemon is remarkable among the undisputed letters of Paul, for it addresses an individual, not a church. The letter deals with a "personal" problem, the fate of the runaway slave Onesimus. The letter is not, however, entirely private; we find that Paul wrote the letter with Timothy. He and Timothy greet not only Philemon but also Apphia, Archippus, and the congregation that meets in Philemon's house. Apparently Paul assumed that the letter would be read at a meeting of the church.

Onesimus, a slave who belonged to Philemon, fled from his master and made his way to Paul who was in prison. Paul converted Onesimus who subsequently was very helpful to Paul. A close relationship developed between Paul and Onesimus, but at the time of the writing Paul was returning Onesimus to his master, an act in strict compliance with Roman law concerning runaway slaves. In this letter to Philemon, Paul intercedes in Onesimus' behalf.

Structure. Our reading comprises the salutation (vv. 1-3), the thanksgiving (vv. 4-7), and the body of the letter (vv. 8-21). The lectionary does not call for the reading of the letter's parenesis (v. 22) or its closing (vv. 23-25), although adding four more verses to the lesson will not prolong the reading significantly. Within the parts of the letter there are subparts and themes, which independently or collectively may inspire proclamation.

Significance. Paul practically convenes a meeting in the salutation of his letter to Philemon. Alongside Paul stands Timothy, and as he addresses Philemon he calls on Apphia, Archippus, and the whole church that meets in Philemon's home. The people Paul calls together know and relate to one another because God moves in their lives. Indeed their very identities as Paul recognizes them—prisoner, brother, sister, fellow soldier, church—are the results of the operation of God among them. Paul's pronouncement of "grace and peace" recognizes the foundation and character of Christian life; grace operates and peace exists because Paul and those whom he addresses experience the presence and power of God in their lives as God works among them and they live under the Lordship of Christ Jesus.

As Paul writes the thanksgiving of his letter to Philemon we get a glimpse of his theology of prayer. For Paul prayer is a regular activity, yet there is a freshness and spontaneity implied in his words. It is as if through prayer Paul took himself into the presence of God and there his innermost self welled up and made itself known to, or better—was known by God. Paul's expression of thanks relates to a concrete memory of what God had been at work doing among others in the church. Remembering Philemon's gracious generosity moved Paul to thank God, for the apostle knew that God was the source of all good in our lives. Paul "prays it safe," hoping for an increase of Philemon's awareness of and obedience to God's will—the very things he thanked God for doing—but now he asks for these in fuller measure. There is a refreshing realism in Paul's prayer of hope. Paul trusts God, thanking God for what has been done and hoping for more of the same.

In the body of the letter Paul makes a subtle appeal for Onesimus. In two places Paul forms word plays on the name Onesimus, a common name among slaves that meant "useful." First, Paul puns the meaning of this Greek name in v. 11 when he says that before Onesimus ("Useful") ran away, he was "useless" (Greek, *achrēstos*); but now that Onesimus is a Christian and is returning, he is "really useful" (Greek, *euchrēstos*). The root in both words is *chrēstos,* which means "useful" or "serviceable." *Chrēstos* was itself a name frequently given to slaves, but here this stem probably plays on the name or title "Christ" (Greek, *Christos*). The prefixes *a-* and *eu-* modify the stem *(chrēstos),* *a-* indicating "without" and *eu-* indicating "good" or "well." Thus, Paul probably means to imply that prior to being a Christian (that is, "without Christ" = *a-christos*) Onesimus ("Useful") was "useless" *(achrēstos),* but as a good Christian *(eu-christos)* formerly useless Onesimus is "really useful" *(euchrēstos).* Second, Paul tells Philemon in v. 20 that he wants some "benefit" *(onaimēn)* from him. While "benefit" and "Onesimus" are not similar in English, *Onesimos* and *onaimēn* look and sound similar in Greek. Thus, using *paronomasia* Paul implies that he desires Onesimus from Philemon.

One other play on words also makes clear what Paul thinks Philemon should do. In v. 7 Paul says "the hearts of the saints have been refreshed through [Philemon]." Then, in v. 12 Paul says that Onesimus is his "very heart." Finally, in v. 20 Paul declares what "benefit" he desires from Onesimus, namely that Philemon "refresh [Paul's] heart in Christ." Paul calls on Philemon, that Christian heart-refresher, to refresh his (Paul's) heart in Christ, and Paul's heart is none other than Onesimus the slave, himself now "in Christ."

The Gospel: *Luke 14:25-33*

The Costs of Discipleship

Setting. As we follow Luke's account of Jesus' journey to Jerusalem, which began at 9:51 and continues through 19:27, we move through a series of three major sections of the story (9:51–13:21; 13:22–17:10; 17:11–19:27). Each section is thematically unified, although the larger blocks of material have several subsections. Our lesson for this Sunday comes in the second major section which is concerned with the deliverance of the lost. The opening words of v. 25 establish the narrative in time, that large crowds followed Jesus, and that he spoke to them. This beginning sets the following verses in such a way that we should see 14:25-35 as a coherent unit of material. While our lesson probably stops two verses short of the actual ending of Luke's intended block of material, this deletion causes no problem and the suggested verses of the lesson are still complex and challenging for preaching.

Structure. Verse 25 provides the context in which we are to understand Jesus' teachings. Then, vv. 26-27 issue a series of startling statements about the ultimate importance of discipleship to Christ. In turn, we encounter two parabolic teachings: first, vv. 28-30 reveal the necessity of single-minded devotion to Christ; second, vv. 31-32 state the necessity of prudent and decisive action in relation to a critical moment. Finally, v. 33 returns in summary fashion to declare the ultimate character of a call to Christian discipleship. The parts of this lesson are united by the urgent, ultimate tone of Jesus' words. As the preacher works with the ideas and themes of these verses, he or she should constantly recall Jesus' demanding demeanor and, thus, formulate a bold call to contemporary discipleship.

Significance. As the crowd came to Jesus he recognized and spoke to the situation, "whoever comes to me." His words make it clear that making casual or merely curious disciples was not his goal in ministry. Jesus confronts the crowd with the stringent demands of genuine discipleship. A true relationship with Jesus Christ means that disciples relativize all other relationships and concerns. Neither one's own family nor one's own life may take precedence over the demands of a relationship to Christ. Indeed, one may infer from Jesus' teachings here that valid family relations and a proper manner of life are only possible when one gives Christ's own program first place. Jesus' language is hyperbolic and, therefore, difficult; but in wrestling with these stern statements we must be careful not to reduce the very real demands that Jesus' teachings place upon those who desire to be his disciples. The cross was more than a metaphor for Jesus, and its cruel demands illustrate perfectly the ultimate, life-demanding character of discipleship. The call to discipleship may come freely in grace, but the cost of discipleship is great, not cheap.

The language and the parables of this lesson are highly eschatological. In vv. 28-30 Jesus speaks of the all-demanding nature of discipleship by telling a story about building a tower. His point: Don't start the difficult work of discipleship unless you intend and are able to complete what you start. Otherwise your failure makes a bad joke of you and the task of discipleship. Then, in vv. 31-32 Jesus uses the violent images of waging war to tell his listeners that disciples must live with an eye to the sure outcome of life. Disciples are to form their lives in relation to their future expectations. If we believe that in Christ God has revealed the character of the future, especially the outcome or end of God's work, then, we should recognize that God has laid a claim on our lives. We are to live now according to God's standards. We live now, despite all difficulties, in terms of God's will. We live now as we shall live in God's future, and while there may be grave consequences for such living, disciples can do nothing other than obey God's will.

In case the listeners (and readers) have not grasped Jesus' point, v. 33 bluntly states the thrust of the foregoing lines. Perhaps this final line should inform and direct the development of a sermon dealing with the total lesson. If there is anything — possessions, life itself, family — that is more important than is our discipleship to Jesus, then we have not weighed the costs of discipleship and taken seriously the outcome of God's work in Jesus Christ. Half-hearted discipleship is not discipleship, we must recognize this disturbing teaching; then, perhaps in honesty we can ask how we may become more faithful followers of Jesus Christ.

Proper 18: The Celebration

See comments in the introduction about the relation of today's lessons to a Labor Day theme. The identification of Jesus as the son of a carpenter might be included in one or more of the liturgical formulae, so the salutation before the opening prayer might be, "May Jesus Christ, the carpenter's son, be with you all." Or the opening prayer might conclude, "Through Jesus Christ, the carpenter's son." A litany of blessing on the various forms of work done by those in the congregation can be composed with the response, "Jesus, son of the carpenter, bless our labors." (Remember that a litany is a prayer with short, repetitive responses after each petition.) Tools and other instruments representative of the diverse occupations in church and community can be used in today's visuals. The following opening prayer incorporates images from all three lessons.

> O God, you work patiently to mold us into your likeness.
> Help us to take seriously the cost of discipleship
> and so carry our crosses in love
> that we may be useful servants
> of the Gospel of Jesus Christ, the carpenter's son. Amen.

Psalm 139:18 is the basis for the hymn by Harriet Beecher Stowe, "Still, Still With Thee." It is absent from most recent hymnals, but is easily found in older editions. The first stanza can serve as an introit either by the choir or a solo voice, or it can be a sung orison before the pastoral prayer or intercessions. The last phrase of the hymn could also be used as the sung response to the major sections of the psalm.

Paul's letter to Philemon serves as an illustration within Scripture itself of how God continues to mold the clay that contains the Gospel treasure. At one level it may be read to portray Paul conservatively conforming to the law of his day, a law that required the return of a runaway slave, and there is no doubt that it has frequently been invoked as a justification for the institution of slavery. But on another level it can be seen as sowing the seeds that would grow into the plant that wrapped itself around the edifice of human bondage and across the centuries ate into the mortar that held it together until the whole structure had to fall. The clay vessel that held the message that baptism radically alters our relationships had to break under the impact of the consequences of that message, and so the church and society continue to experience the formative fingers of God as they etch new configurations for our life together.

The following Wesley stanza (tune: St. Catherine) is a fitting response at the offertory or to the benediction, since it draws upon the clay image from Jeremiah, the baptismal ("stamp") reference from Philemon, and the singleness of purpose from Luke.

> Here then to thee thine own I leave;
> > Mould as thou wilt thy passive clay;
> But let me all thy stamp receive,
> > But let me all thy words obey;
> Serve with a single heart and eye,
> And to thy glory live and die.

(*Hymns and Psalms* [London: Methodist Publishing House, 1983], no. 788.)

Proper Nineteen Sunday Between September 11 and 17 Inclusive

Old Testament Texts

Jeremiah 4:11-12, 22-28 presents a vision of cosmic destruction. Psalm 14 is a lament about the foolishness of humans.

The Lesson: *Jeremiah 4:11-12, 22-28*

The Undoing of Creation

Setting. The lectionary reading has pieced together several sections of an account of destruction that includes at least Jeremiah 4:5-31. More precisely, the unit is a description of judgment, conceived of as a foe from the north. Verse 6 reads, "Raise a standard toward Zion flee for safety, do not delay for I am bringing evil from the north, and a great destruction." The "I" of this speech is God. Thus the foe from the north is a form of divine punishment. Yet the identity of this foe is unclear. The foe from the north may be historical, in which case the Babylonian invasion of Judah is being conceived as a divine punishment. Verses 5-8 support a historical reading of the foe from the north, because of the prominence of the imagery of warfare.

Two responses to invasion are presented in vv. 9-12. The first (vv. 9-10) is the response of Judah's leaders to invasion; the king, leaders, priests, and prophets will all be astounded at the destruction. The second response (vv. 11-12) focuses on the people in general. They will be overcome by the destructive force of the hot summer wind, which will destroy indiscriminately. The two responses give way to further descriptions of the invading army and the divine pronouncement that it is a form of judgment (vv. 13-18) before language of lament takes over in vv. 19-22. The foe from the north takes on cosmic proportions in vv. 23-28 when destruction transcends the nation of Judah and begins to dismantle creation itself. This overview of the larger section of 4:5-31 underscores how God is behind the activity of the foe from the north as a form of punishment against Judah and how the foe is both historical and cosmological. The lectionary reading focuses on the cosmological dimensions of God's punishment.

Structure. The lectionary reading is made up of several distinct sections of the larger unit, which explore the relationship between God and the people of Israel (vv. 11-12, 22) and the effects of this relationship on the entire created order (vv. 23-28).

Significance. Religion and the life of faith are not simply matters of the heart as is so often implied in contemporary religious piety. Jeremiah 4 provides an excellent occasion for the preacher to explore how the life of faith is inextricably linked to the larger order of the creation. In Jeremiah 4 the relationship between God and the people of God has a direct bearing on the well-being of the entire creation. The text explores the cosmological implications of human sin.

Verses 11-12, 22 focus on the relationship between God and the people of God. Commentators disagree on whether the speaker is God or Jeremiah in vv. 11-12. The present reading assumes God to be the speaker. The point of the verses is that the hot desert wind, known as the sirocco, is a form of judgment on Israel. It has no redeeming characteristic such as a source for winnowing. When read in the larger context, the destructive sirocco wind would seem to be commentary on the foe from the north. The judgment that will accompany this foe has no redeeming characteristics. Verse 22 separates from the preceding lament in vv. 19-21 in tone. Verses 19-21 appear to be the prophet's anguished reaction to the impending judgment, while a more distant voice enters in v. 22 to provide a reason for the judgment. The language of v. 22 is reminiscent of wisdom tradition with the divine speaker in the role of a wisdom teacher. The reason for the absolute judgment without any hope of redemption is that Israel is stupid and foolish (Hebrew, *èwil*—which one commentator translates as "blockheaded"). The source of their stupidity is that they do not know God.

Verses 23-28 explore how Israel's stupidity can spill over and contaminate all of creation. Verses 23-26 separate into four visions by the prophet ("I looked . . . "). These visions go beyond the destruction of Judah to its effects on the larger creation. The background of the prophet's apocalyptic visions is most certainly some form of Genesis 1. Especially noteworthy in this regard is the description of the earth as being "waste and void" in v. 23. This is the description of pre-creation chaos in Genesis 1:2. The innerbiblical connection suggests that the prophet's series of visions in vv. 23-26 are about the undoing of created order: earth dissolves into chaos; the lights of heaven are put out; the mountains and hills, which support creation, are removed with the result that life in the air (birds) on land (fruitful trees) and in society (cities) is extinguished. Verses 27-28 appear to provide a qualification to the total annihilation of creation. But a firm interpretation is difficult at this point, since the qualification is limited to v. 27, while v. 28 actually moves in the other direction and underscores the relentlessness with which God would bring total destruction on the creation. The conflict in these verses reflects debate by the writers of Jeremiah concerning the degree to which God would allow the creation to be undone on the basis of Israel's sin.

To the writers of the book of Jeremiah religion is not simply a matter of the heart. For them the life of faith has consequences that may influence the very structure of creation itself.

The Response: Psalm 14

Fools

Setting. Psalm 14 is repeated in Psalm 53. Scholars speculate that perhaps the duplication arises from distinctive books that have come together in the present form of the psalter. There are some textual differences between the two psalms, with the most pronounced being the use of Lord in Psalm 14 as compared to God in Psalm 53. The duplication raises interesting questions concerning the formation of the psalter, but unfortunately it provides no assistance in interpreting the psalm. Some see prophetic influence in the psalm with the opening verses functioning as an invective or judgment.

Others emphasize the language of wisdom and thus so locate the psalm with overtones of lament. Both options provide points of contact with Jeremiah 4:11-12, 22-28.

Structure. The psalm separates into three parts. Verses 1-4 explore the thoughts of the fool over against God's perception of them from heaven. Verses 5-6 sketch out the fate of the fool over against that of the righteous. Finally v. 7 is a wishful sigh or glance at a future salvation.

Significance. The language of foolishness stands out when Psalm 14 is read as a response to Jeremiah 4. Of particular note is the assessment of Israel as being foolish in v. 22. With this starting point, Psalm 14 is best read as a lament or prophetic announcement concerning the fate of the fool. The most striking characteristic of the fool is his or her conclusion in v. 1 that God is absent ("There is no God"). When the reader follows the structure of the psalm this opening affirmation by the fool is in fact a true assessment of the fool's life. God is not located with the fool, but in heaven. Furthermore, it is this absence of God in their daily (or perhaps better cultic) life that actually defines them as being foolish. This stupidity was also true of Jeremiah 4:22. The prophet described the people of Israel as being "blockheads" because they did not know God. In Psalm 14 God enters the world of humans in vv. 5-6, which has two consequences. For the fool it is terror, but for the righteous it is refuge. The psalmist identifies with the righteous in v. 7 by wishfully hoping for God's salvation in the present time.

New Testament Texts

At a glance the complex, but coherent, lines of the reading from I Timothy appear to be a departure from the line of thought articulated in the first portion of the letter, especially vv. 3-11. But examination of the reading reveals that the seeming aside is, in fact, a rich meditation on the "glorious gospel of the blessed God" mentioned in v. 11. The Gospel lesson brings our attention to two of the three (or four) parables in the famous fifteenth chapter of Luke. Naming these parables is a challenge and says much about the point of view one takes on the stories. The first parable is best known as the story of "the lost sheep," but its real subject is "the faithful, searching shepherd"; the second parable is known as the story of "the lost coin," but the central character is actually "the diligent, searching sweeper."

The Epistle: *I Timothy 1:12-17*

God's Mercy and the Purposes of Salvation in Christ Jesus

Setting. The opening chapter of I Timothy establishes the occasion for the letter, revealing that there are false teachers whose work and teaching are to be opposed by those with correct theological sensibilities and correspondingly pure lives. After the salutation (1:1-2) at the beginning of a Hellenistic letter, this epistle omits the normal statement of thanksgiving that follows the greeting and precedes the body of the letter. Rather, in I Timothy the author moves directly from the salutation to the body of the work in 1:3. Our reading for this Sunday, however, opens with words similar to those that might begin an epistolary thanksgiving, "I am grateful to Christ Jesus our Lord . . . "; although this word of thanks introduces a very personal doxological declaration about God's glory revealed in the coming of Christ Jesus into the world to save sinners (vv. 12-17).

Structure. There are four major parts to this reading. The first segment has two parts. Verses 12-13 offer thanksgiving for the transformation and commissioning of Paul the persecutor of the church into Paul the agent of God's ministry of salvation. Second, v. 14 continues to meditate on the grace that was embodied in the faith and love of Christ Jesus himself. Verses 15-16 form a third segment of the reading. The thought moves from personal thanksgiving to expand upon the theme of Christ Jesus coming into the world to save sinful humanity, and the verses continue by saying that the grace experienced by Paul was a demonstration for the benefit of others. Fourth, our reading has moved from thanksgiving to testimony and now it concludes in the praise of God for God's transforming, saving, eternal grace. The structure of thanksgiving, testimony, and praise offer a pattern and dynamic momentum that are suggestive for preaching.

Significance. As the opening thanksgiving and the concluding doxology indicate, this passage focuses intensely on God's saving grace. The personal cast of the language throughout the verses should not lead one astray toward an interpretation of this passage as a simple personal statement expressive of the author's piety. Rather, the author is focused on God and the overwhelming experience of God's grace that profoundly effects the personal faith of all believers. The grace of God for which the author gives thanks and which the author praises is clearly no abstraction, for the references to Christ Jesus identify the very real historical and human dimensions of God's grace. Grace here means salvation for human sinners as the bold teaching of v. 15 reveals.

The dominant pattern of New Testament thanksgivings is that they are offered to God, whereas the opening verse of our reading offers thanks to Christ Jesus. One should notice the cast of the thanks: Christ Jesus is not thanked abstractly, but specifically, for strengthening or energizing Paul by reckoning him faithful and, in turn, for setting him about the doing of ministry. Thanks goes to Christ Jesus for the transformation of life—as we learn from the lesson—from a life of disbelieving ignorance to a life of faithful ministry. Grace alters our lives from faithlessness to faithfulness, from disobedience to obedience, from resistance to God's will to the doing of God's work under God's direction. God reckons neither sinful ignorance nor ignorant sinfulness against those to whom God extends grace in Christ Jesus. God reforms sinful life into an active life of service to God's saving grace.

At the heart of our reading and at the heart of this meditation on grace is the clear conviction that the saving work of God transpires in and through the person of Christ Jesus. As the mediator of God's grace to sinners, Christ Jesus is himself the locus and well-spring of faith and love. The faithful service of Christ Jesus in bearing the love of God into the world to save sinners both was the origin of faith and is the source of faith that means that sinners obtain the mercy of God.

Furthermore, from this reading we learn that a central purpose in God's transformation of sinners into those who experience grace is for the redirection of life in the work of ministry. The reading explains that Paul became a showcase of God's mercy as he was altered from a life of grave opposition to God's work to a life of steadfast service to Christ Jesus. Others could see concretely the results of God's mercy as they observed the course of Paul's life. As Christ Jesus mediated faith and love to sinners, Paul's very person provided bold testimony to the purpose and power of God's grace. Because of this change and this life of service we find v. 17 offering lofty praise to God's eternal glory.

The Gospel: *Luke 15:1-10*

Symbols of the Extent of God's Love

Setting. Luke's account of Jesus' journey to Jerusalem is long, and along the way one can forget that the trip has begun and that there is a destination in view. In the fifteenth chapter, as Jesus makes his way toward his forthcoming Passion, Luke recalls parables that Jesus told to his listeners. The audience is mixed. So-called tax collectors and sinners gather about Jesus as do the Pharisees and scribes. The tax-collectors and sinners seem drawn to Jesus by his openness to them, which is evident in his mighty works and deeds, but the Pharisees and scribes are portrayed as Jesus' critics, even as his adversaries. Luke's reader observes the mixed audience with its different dispositions toward Jesus, and with both groups in view, as Luke's readers, we listen to Jesus as he tells two stories about being lost and found or about searching for that which is lost.

Structure. Interpreters frequently point out that Luke 15 comprises two double parables: (1) vv. 4-7 and vv. 8-10; and (2) vv. 11-24 and vv. 25-32. The second set of stories is clearly more connected that the first pair of parables, although in their form the stories in vv. 4-7 and 8-10 are repetitious.

In our lesson vv. 1-2 establish the setting. Tax-collectors and sinners came to hear Jesus and the Pharisees and the scribes criticized Jesus' receiving these people and even eating with them. Verse 3 works the transition from setting to story: With fans and critics present, Jesus told parables. The stories are different, but the language and the structure of the parables are remarkably similar.

Beginning:	What man having . . . (v. 4).
	What woman having . . . (v. 8).
Development:	Loss (vv. 4, 8).
Action:	Leave . . . until he finds it (v. 4).
	Sweep and seek . . . until she finds it (v. 8).
Result:	Rejoicing (vv. 5, 9)
Explanation:	Likewise, joy in heaven over one repentant sinner (v. 7).
	Likewise, joy among God's angels over one repentant sinner (v. 10).

The ending explanations control the reading of the parables. Since the heavenly joy over each repentant sinner is being illustrated in the parables, the shepherd and the sweeper seem to symbolize God's manner of dealing with sinners.

Significance. The parables tell us that God cares for all humanity, for all one hundred sheep and for all ten coins. The assembled ninety-nine sheep or the nine coins do not obscure God's universal vision that sees each human in her or his own condition. This initial observation tells us the heart of the good news of God's love.

Along with this good news, however, comes somewhat less pleasant information. The parables tell us that individuals become lost, separated from God's care, guidance, and grace. Moreover, while one does not want to treat the parables as if they were allegories, the details of the stories are worth pondering for the wealth of suggestive information that they give us for theological reflection. Indeed, the images of the parables tell us that this condition of lostness is simultaneously a condition of estrangement from God and other humans, for the sheep and the coin were lost from the other sheep and the other coins as well as from the shepherd and the sweeper.

Yet, because God does care, God seeks out the lost, or as the concluding lines to both parables call such humans, God seeks out sinners. Here is the nature of lostness. Sin is life out of touch with and contrary to God's will. We are lost to God as we turn away from God's purposes and pursue our own agendas and goals that are not set or established in relation to God. In turn, it is remarkable that

37

being found by God means that previously lost, sinful humans become repentant. The parables speak of a great mystery, namely that God cares for us in our lostness, that as we are lost in sin God seeks us out. Because God grasps our lives, rescuing us from lostness, we are transformed from lives of sin to become repentant sinners with a new divinely constituted relationship to God.

In the context of Luke's Gospel we should see that God pursues humanity in the person and work of Jesus Christ. Like the shepherd in pursuit of his beloved but lost sheep and like the sweeper in search of her precious lost coin, God in Jesus Christ relentlessly pursues us to bring us through repentance out of lostness and into fellowship with God and God's people.

One final suggestive detail in these parables is worth pondering for proclamation. The shepherd searched, not until dark, but until he found the sheep; the woman swept, not until her broom gave out, but until she found the coin. Does God in Jesus Christ pursue us likewise, until we are found and reclaimed for God's own purposes?

Proper 19: The Celebration

The commentary above on Jeremiah points out that "the relationship between God and the people of God has a direct bearing on the well-being of the entire creation." As we begin to make the transition between seasons, it is a good time to reaffirm our relationship with creation as a part of our covenant with God, and to examine the nature and consequences of how we have conducted that relationship. The eight hottest summers on record have occurred since 1980 (see v. 11), and the birds of the air have not so much fled (v. 25) as they have been decimated by the pollutants poured into the air and water and the merciless appropriation of their nesting grounds by the ever expanding human population. Are these facts in any way signs of the foolishness of God's people who in their technological advances have become "skilled in doing evil"? It is as easy to wax merely sentimental about nature as it is to be callously indifferent and whistle in the dark that nature always rights itself and that human demands always come first.

The preacher needs to avoid both the pitfall of preaching ecological apocalypticism on the one hand and that of anthropocentric ecology on the other. Some background reading essential to an informed approach to the issues should include Bill McKibben's *The End of Nature* (New York: Doubleday, 1989); Thomas Berry's *Befriending the Earth: A Theology of Reconciliation between Humans and the Earth* (Mystic, Conn.: Twenty-Third Publications, 1991); James Nash's *Loving Nature: Ecological Integrity and Christian Responsibility* (Nashville: Abingdon Press, 1991); and Dieter T. Hessel, ed., *For Creation's Sake: Preaching, Ecology, and Justice* (Philadelphia: Geneva Press, 1985). Various denominations are now publishing more liturgical resources that represent ecological awareness. Two additional collections of value are Elizabeth Roberts and Elias Amidon, *Earth Prayers from Around the World* (San Francisco: Harper San Francisco, 1991) and Susan J. Clark, *Celebrating Earth Holy Days: A Resource Guide for Faith Communities* (New York: Crossroad, 1992). Related "children's moments" materials may be found in *Our Children, Their Earth: Playing for Keeps*, by the United Nations Environment Programme (The United Nations, New York, NY 10017). It is noteworthy that Psalm 14 underscores the justice issues related to the poverty that is caused by the imperatives of a technological society that concentrates power and decision making in the hands of an ever smaller elite. See John Cobb Jr., *Sustainability: Economics, Ecology, and Justice* (Maryknoll, N.Y.: Orbis, 1992).

I Timothy 1:17 is the source for the hymn, "Immortal, Invisible, God Only Wise," a fitting opening hymn for this day because of its references to the natural order as well.

We find ready references in the poetry of Charles Wesley to the Gospel lesson, and they are pertinent to different acts of worship throughout the service.

As an introit or call to prayer, the following long meter text:

> O thou whom once they flocked to hear,
> thy words to hear, thy power to feel;
> suffer the sinners to draw near,
> and graciously receive us still.

As a response to the reading of the Gospel, either this long meter text:

> Ready for you the angels wait,
> to triumph in your blest estate;
> tuning their harps, they long to praise
> the wonders of redeeming grace.

or this 88.88.88 meter text:

> Sinners, believe the gospel word,
> Jesus is come your souls to save!
> Jesus is come, your common Lord!
> Pardon ye all in him may have,
> may now be saved, whoever will;
> this man receiveth sinners still.

At the Confession of Sin, these 88.88.88 meter lines may be used after a time of silent recollection and before the Declaration of Pardon:

> How shall I find the living way,
> lost, and confused, and dark, and blind?
> Ah, Lord, my soul is gone astray;
> ah, Shepherd, seek my soul, and find,
> and in thy arms of mercy take,
> and bring the weary wanderer back.

The old gospel hymn, "The Ninety and Nine," is absent from many recent hymnals, but may still be found in increasingly rare copies of the 1935 *Methodist Hymnal* and in the independent hymnal *Favorite Hymns of Praise* (Chicago: Tabernacle, 1967). The dramatic Sankey tune was composed expressly for the text written by Elizabeth Clephane, and it is admirably fitted for a male solo voice, or it can be arranged for a male chorus. Robert McCutchan, in his commentary on the hymn, said that "Probably no other gospel song has ever been more popular." If that is the case, it is to be regretted that it has almost vanished without a trace from the contemporary gospel song repertoire.

Proper Twenty Sunday Between September 18 and 24 Inclusive

Old Testament Texts

Jeremiah 8:18-9:1 is a lamentation over the destruction of Judah. Psalms 79:1-9 is a psalm of lament.

The Lesson: *Jeremiah 8:18–9:1*

A Lamentation over Jerusalem

Setting. The form-critical designation of Jeremiah 8:18–9:1 as a lamentation is clear. We do not know, however, who is lamenting. Many commentators suggest the voice of the prophet Jeremiah. Thus first person references like "my joy," "my heart," "my people," or "I mourn" are references to the prophet. Most would agree that even if the prophet is designated as the speaker, the lamentation is meant to be communal in nature, so that the prophet actually represents the community.

It is also possible that either certain parts or perhaps even all of the lamentation is the voice of God. Several reasons can be given to support such a reading. First, God is certainly the speaker in the larger context. Note how the preceding verses (8:16-17) are clearly a speech of God ("See, I am letting snakes loose among you, . . . and they shall bite you, says the LORD.") and how the following verses (9:2-3) are also clearly a speech of God ("They bend their tongues like bows . . . and they do not know me, says the LORD.") Second, God is most likely the speaker in v. 19*b* ("Why have they provoked me to anger with their images, with their foreign idols?") And third, the first person references to "my [poor] people" in 8:19, 21, 22, and 9:1 are used in divine speech in 9:2. So who is lamenting for whom in this text?

41

Structure. The text separates into three parts: 8:18, 8:19-21, and 8:22–9:1. The opening verse (8:18) establishes the mood of lamentation, without identifying the speaker. The second section (8:19-21) is complicated in structure. It begins (8:19) by signaling how the following material will be a quotation from the people ("Hark, the cry of my poor people from far and wide in the land"). What actually follows, however, is both quotation and a response by the speaker. The people are quoted as saying two things: (1)"Is the LORD not in Zion: Is her King not in her?" (v. 19); and (2) "The harvest is past, the summer is ended, and we are not saved" (v. 20). Sandwiched between these two quotations is the voice of the speaker, "Why have they provoked me to anger with their images, with their foreign idols?" (v. 9*b*). The second section ends in 8:21 with the speaker participating in the pain of the people. The third section (8:22–9:1) presents a flurry or rhetorical questions that evolve into an unfulfillable wish that the speaker might weep for the lost people. The text can be outlined in the following manner:

    I.   Cry of Lamentation (8:18)
    II.   Quotation from the People with Response by Speaker
         (8:19-21)
        A. First Quotation: Is the Lord not in Zion?
        B. First Response: Why have they provoked me to anger?
        A. Second Quotation: The harvest is past . . . we are not
           saved.
        B. Second Response: I am hurt . . . I mourn.
    III. An unfulfillable Wish (8:22-9:1)

Significance. The preacher is forced to determine who is lamenting whom. Perhaps the prophet (or later redactors who speak through the persona of the prophet) is lamenting the destruction of the southern kingdom. In this interpretation the prophet presents the opening cry of lamentation, recounts first the central confession of Israel that God dwelt in Zion and would never leave it, but as a question of doubt rather than a statement of fact. The doubt is confirmed in the second quotation, when the community concludes that summer is past and, indeed, salvation is not on the horizon.

The voice of the prophet returns at the conclusion when he embodies the suffering of the people and wishes against all hope that restoration would be possible. This interpretation (of prophetic and communal lamentation over the lose of God) requires that the first response be overlooked, because the voice in this response is clearly God's. This disruption of the internal logic of the lament (from a prophetic speaker to God) has prompted scholars to suggest that the first response is a later addition. They suggest that it may be commentary to account for the fall of the kingdom. Some commentators like William McKane (*Jeremiah: A Critical and Exegetical Commentary,* The International Critical Commentary [Edinburg: T and T Clark, 1986]) go so far as to remove the response from the text altogether.

A second reading would move in just the other direction and use the addition as the point of departure for interpretation. In this case the insertion of divine speech raises the question of whether all the unmarked first person references (for example, *I* and *my*) might not also be the voice of God. A very different interpretation arises, for the lamentation is now by God over the loss of Israel. Thus, it is God who introduces the opening cry, and who recounts Israel's bewilderment over their destruction, "Is the LORD not in Zion?" The divine response answers the question: God is not in Zion, because Israel has driven God away. The tone of the divine response, however, is wishful thinking in the form of a question—"Why have they provoked me?"—and the remainder of the lament then develops a theology of divine suffering. God hurts with the people. God wonders if there is any balm that might help? And in the end God can only wish for unfound depths of lamentation.

Both of the previous readings are central for preaching this text in its present form. Redactors have transformed a prophetic lament over a fallen nation or, if read collectively, a national lament over the loss of God, into a cosmology in which lamentation becomes part of the very character of God, with the result that God laments the loss of Israel. Thus the text probes the profound implications of our choices. It suggests that some choices are so profound that once they are made, they can ever lock God into the role of lamenter rather than savior, regardless of how much the divine may wish otherwise.

The Response: *Psalm 79:1-9*

A Lament

Setting. Psalm 79:1-9 continues the mood of lamentation from Jeremiah 8:18–9:1, but removes all ambiguity about who is speaking. This is clearly a lament by the community, which presently experiences the absence of God in their midst.

Structure. Psalm 79 separates into two or three parts. Verses 1-4 present a complaint to God, vv. 5-12 shift to the language of petition, and v. 13 is a conclusion expressing confidence in God. The lectionary reading stops midway through the petition, with the call for help in v. 9.

Significance. When Psalm 79 is read as a response to Jeremiah 8:18–9:1, all the world becomes an echo chamber of lamenting voices. Very little light or hope can be experienced in these lectionary readings. In such situations, the act of lamenting is therapeutic, for it at least it keeps the conversation going. People who cease lamenting are people who have given up hope for a better day.

New Testament Texts

The epistle reading takes up the important topic of prayer, particularly the proper subject(s) of prayer. The Christian belief in one God who is known in and through Jesus Christ directs believers to a life of prayer that includes all persons, for God is the one God of all. The Gospel lesson presents one of Jesus' strangest parables and a set of statements that aim at unpacking the meaning of the surprising story of the unjust steward. The lesson challenges Christians to be shrewd, not dishonest, as they strive to live faithfully in this world.

The Epistle: *I Timothy 2:1-7*

Praying for the Right Things

Setting. Readers may consult the discussion of the setting of the epistle reading for last Sunday to gain fuller information about I Timothy. After the first chapter, the epistle continues by offering a set of pointed directions in 2:1–3:13. Commentators regularly refer to

2:1–3:13 as a brief church leadership manual. The first distinguishable unit of guidelines in this larger section is our epistle lesson. These verses are a statement about prayer, and they are concerned with the objects of prayer and with the theological basis of appropriate praying. Further teaching about prayer, essentially declaring what is proper deportment in prayer, comes in 2:8-15. After these two sections on praying, I Timothy treats the qualification of church leaders and, then, returns to the issue of false teachers.

Structure. One clear thread runs through this whole paragraph and holds it together—namely, the author's regularly repeated conviction that the gospel and the life of Christian faith are concerned with all human beings (see vv. 1, 4, and 6). This unifying interest, however, should not obscure the motion of the author's thought in these verses. First, the author calls for prayer for everyone (v. 1). Second, he digresses momentarily to focus the need for prayer specifically in relation to leaders of all kinds; yet even this prayer is for the well being of all (v. 2). Third, in vv. 3-4 we find that such prayer is pleasing to God, and we learn that the God who accepts such praying is the one who desires for all persons to be saved and to know the truth. Fourth, this theological verification of the call to prayer for all persons is itself validated by the inclusion of what interpreters judge to be a creedal statement in vv. 5-6. And, fifth, we learn that the apostle Paul was appointed to instruct the Gentiles in matters of faith and truth because of God's concern for the welfare of all humans (v. 7).

Significance. In a nutshell, this lesson is a call to prayer for a life of peace and godliness for all humanity as they are established in faith and truth according to the will of God. God's purposes were made known and active by and through Jesus Christ and, now, in the continuing ministry of the apostle. This is a large, complex, but single idea.

Above all, Christians may be thankful that God wills and works for the salvation of all persons. Salvation means that because of what God has done in Jesus Christ (the message born by the Church to the rest of the world) humans are being brought to faith and to a knowledge of God's truth. The result of the advent of faith and truth in the lives of humans is that their manner of life is transformed.

Persons of faith and truth lead respectable, godly, peaceful lives. This means that order is restored to human existence as humans are brought together under the saving grace of Jesus Christ. This harmony among humans is genuinely expressive of the oneness of God, who through Jesus Christ has grasped a once-fragmented humanity and brought them together with himself into the context of the new community of faith.

Those who experience and know this saving work of God through Jesus Christ find their lives transformed. And as they orient themselves toward God through prayer, they offer God thanks for what has been and is being done for others (and themselves). A true prayer, combining petition and thanksgiving, will always tend toward praise. It will ask God to do more of what has been done rather than tell God how to be as good as we would be if we were God.

Implicit in this lesson is a denunciation of disorder and particularity that denies and undermines the universal scope of God's concern with all humankind (a stance typical of the false teachers already criticized in chapter 1, and who will be criticized further in the latter portions of the letter). The one God is the God of all, and, in Jesus Christ, God acts to reunite humans with one another as through Christ they are reunited with God. For this we give God thanks in prayer.

The Gospel: *Luke 16:1-13*

Living Shrewdly Because of God

Setting. Having spoken in parables (chapter 15) to the crowds that came to hear him, Jesus turns at the beginning of chapter 16 to his disciples with further parabolic teaching. Our lesson is a complex of verses clustered about the parable of the unjust steward. One verse of the lesson, v. 13, has a parallel in Matthew 6:24, a part of the Sermon on the Mount. The parable itself (vv. 1-8a) and the series of sayings that follow (vv. 8b-12) are unparalleled elsewhere in the New Testament. Thus, scholars conclude that v. 13 is Q material, but the parable and the other sayings are special Lukan traditions, although it is not impossible that portions of vv. 8b-12 were also in the Q source.

Structure. Verse 1a quickly focuses Jesus' teaching in relation to the disciples. The parable of the unjust steward then runs from v. 1b through v. 7. Scholars increasingly understand that the statement in v. 8a, "The master [literally, 'the Lord'] . . . for his shrewdness" (my translation), to be Luke's narrative report of Jesus' own evaluation of the unjust steward. The NRSV is inaccurate and misleading in rending the beginning of v. 8, "And his master." Elsewhere in Luke's special materials and in his narration of the gospel account, the Lord refers to Jesus himself—see, for example, 7:13; 10:39-41; 13:15; 18:6; 19:8; 22:61; 24:34. The ensuing remarks in vv. 8b-13 "add to" the original report in v. 8a by repeating the word *hoti* in Greek (meaning, "for" or "because"), so that the explanation of Jesus' praise of the unjust steward is expanded by recording loosely related sayings from Jesus himself.

In fact, our lesson has several sub-units: vv. 1-8a, 8b, 9, 10-12, 13. In the discussion of significance I shall treat each of these units so that one or several of the sections may provide the basis of a sermon.

Significance. Frequently Jesus' parables are about "the Kingdom of God," so that one hears or reads the parables as explicit stories about God and God's ways. The parables in Luke 13 and 15 are excellent examples of this kind of teaching. The parable of the unjust steward is different from the Kingdom-of-God parables, however, and scholarly attempts to identify explicitly theological themes in this story often fail. This story is not simply an appeal for alms-giving, generosity, forgiveness, or the proper use of wealth; and it is not a criticism of the Jewish religious authorities of Jesus' day. Rather, the story is an eschatological lesson about the urgency of discipleship.

Jesus' disciples are to be shrewd in arranging all facets of their lives in the light of God's revealed will and ways in the person and work of Jesus Christ. In Jesus Christ, God creates a critical moment that demands the radical reordering of life's priorities. Those who have the benefit of Christ's call to discipleship have encountered God's transforming claim on their lives. In this world even a dishonest administrator knows how to rig a golden parachute, and Jesus tells us in this parable that comparable, but appropriate, radical

47

action is now required of disciples who must live toward God's future as God in Jesus Christ requires. Saved by grace through faith may be the essence of the gospel, but if we are listening to Jesus we should hear that grace grasps our lives and transforms us so that faith means we live according to God's will.

The second word of explanation in v. 8b drives home the urgency of a faith-formed existence by criticizing the sad and inexcusable naïveté of the children of light with the dishonest but creative management of life by the children of this age. God calls for action, not merely passive presumption on the goodness of grace.

Verse 9 makes the startling point that the way we live in the present has real consequences for our experience of God's future. The way we live, the values we hold, the relationships we form right now are vitally related to God's future. Thus, God lays a claim on our lives that calls for and offers the transformation of present existence in compliance with God's future.

At a glance vv. 10-12 are strange, particularly v. 12. Yet, when we remember the eschatological cast of this section of Jesus' teachings we can see that being faithful with what belongs to another refers to our stewardship of life and earthly possessions (all things do indeed belong to the Creator); and the reference to receiving what is our own indicates the results of God's judgment and grace in the future, in God's future.

Verse 13 is self-evident. We can either live for God or for material goods, but we cannot live for both. Jesus plainly means to confront confused and self-deceptive thinking and to challenge his disciples to live for God.

Proper 20: The Celebration

The Old Testament lesson calls to mind the African American spiritual, "There Is a Balm in Gilead," which answers positively the question raised by Jeremiah. The spiritual can be used as part of today's Act of Confession and Pardon. After the customary unison prayer of confession and silent recollection, the liturgist reads Jeremiah 18:22, the spiritual is sung in unison, by the choir, or as a solo; and then the Declaration of Pardon is pronounced. The Act of Confession and Pardon could be offered in response to the reading from the Old Testament and the psalm, so that the use of 18:22 would recall what had previously been heard.

It is appropriate that the reading of the people's lament—"The harvest is past, the summer is ended, and we are not saved" (Jeremiah 8:20)—comes during this week when the autumnal equinox will occur. The sequence is different than we know it and has to be understood in terms of the agriculture of Palestine where the harvest occurs in the spring, and the summer is the time when other fruits may still be gathered. If the harvest failed, the summer fruit could serve to ward off famine, but if both failed disaster was at hand. A confession today might examine whether we ignore present duties because we trust in future fruits that may not mature.

The reading from I Timothy provides an opportunity for the worship committee to discuss the nature of public prayer and its purpose in the Christian community. How well do we include everyone in our intercessions? Do the joys and concerns expressed ever get beyond the four walls? This may be the time to remind pastors that their function in the oversight of public prayer is not to scribble down hastily all the intentions raised orally by the congregation and then give them a sacerdotal rubber stamp by repeating them all over again. Their expression by the members is the prayer, and it doesn't need a clerical second. The pastor's job is to see that the whole work of intercession, petition, and thanksgiving is done over a period of time, and to raise those concerns that remain unexpressed by the membership. Thanksgiving is an area where American Christian consciousness needs heightening in particular. Many congregations, while big on concerns, are frequently thin on joys unless they are of an immediate and personal nature. How can the church's prayer help people learn to be thankful for blessings received by others? Note also that the reason given here for praying for rulers is that they are to ensure a peaceable society, and that makes it possible to do the work of evangelization more easily.

For a stimulating interpretation of the story of the unjust servant, preachers are referred to Robert Farrar Capon's *The Parables of Grace* (Grand Rapids, Mich.: Eerdmans, 1988). Briefly put, Father Capon suggests that the unjust servant is a Christ-figure who identifies with the prodigal son who also wasted his living as the servant wasted his master's living and who both experience death either among the pigs or by being dismissed.

> The unjust steward is the Christ-figure because he is a crook, like Jesus. The unique contribution of this parable to our understanding of Jesus is its insistence that grace cannot come to the world through respectability. Respectability regards only life, success, winning; it will have no truck with the grace that works by death and losing — which is the only kind of grace there is. (p. 150)

And Fr. Capon concludes, "Lucky for us we don't have to deal with a just steward."

Wesley's hymn, "A Charge to Keep I Have," is based in part on today's lesson from Luke.

Proper Twenty-one Sunday Between September 25 and October 1 Inclusive

Old Testament Texts

Jeremiah 32:1-3*a*, 6-15 is the account of Jeremiah purchasing a plot of land in his home town of Anathoth while Jerusalem was under siege. Psalm 91 is a liturgy about divine protection in the sanctuary.

The Lesson: *Jeremiah 32:1-3*a, 6-15

Hope under Seige

Setting. Jeremiah 32 is an extended chapter that separates into three parts. Verses 1-15 recount how Jeremiah purchased land during the Babylonian siege of Jerusalem. Thus this section focuses on prophetic action that is meant to symbolize hope.

Structure. Jeremiah 32:1-15 separates into two very distinct parts. Verses 1-5 recount how Jeremiah is under house arrest by King Zedekiah for prophesying about the downfall of Jerusalem during siege warfare. For some unknown reason the lectionary has eliminated a large section of Jeremiah's prophesy by limiting the text to vv. 1-3*a*. The preacher may wish to restore vv. 3*b*-5 to the lectionary reading. Verses 6-15 begin with Jeremiah recounting how his cousin Hanamel came to him (presumably in prison in Jerusalem during siege warfare) and offered him the right to purchase family property in Anathoth.

Significance. The central message of Jeremiah 32:1-15 is hope. Any sermon on this text must (1) explore what hope means to the people of God, (2) how hope influences action, and (3) how the prophet provides the paradigm of the hope-filled person of God. If the account of Jeremiah buying land during the Babylonian siege is the only point of focus, then the message of hope runs the danger of becoming trite. In the face of all odds, the courageous prophet buys land to express his unswerving faith in God. This message, however, is complicated in three ways: by the juxtaposition of vv. 1-5 and 6-15, by the variety of characters that have been included in these few short verses, and by the prayer of Jeremiah in vv. 16-25.

First the juxtaposition of vv. 1-5 and vv. 6-15. The purchase of land does not follow logically from the opening setting. Jeremiah is in jail in vv. 1-5 because he is prophesying a Babylonian victory. The prophet's point of focus is not hope in this section but judgment. The purchase of land in vv. 6-15 immediately following vv. 1-5 makes no sense for a number of reasons. To whom is Jeremiah talking in v. 6? How did his cousin travel from Anathoth when Jerusalem was under siege by the Babylonians? And even if we grant him this miracle, how did he get in to see Jeremiah? What are we to make of these contradictions? At the very least these explicit breaks in narrative logic underscore how hope is neither casual nor reasonable.

Second, there are an unusual number of characters in this contradictory story of hope. There is King Zedekiah fighting for the life of the kingdom; the Babylonian King Nebuchadnezzar in the role of the invader; Jeremiah's cousin Hanamel from Anathoth; and Baruch, who, as Jeremiah's secretary, is charged with preserving the deeds of Jeremiah for posterity. Jeremiah has a complex relationship with all of these characters. He appeared to be against King Zedekiah and for King Nebuchadnezzar in vv. 1-5 by predicting the downfall of Judah but then changes roles in vv. 6-15 with the purchase of land. Earlier Jeremiah was threatened by death from the men of Anathoth (11:21-23), yet in vv. 6-15 Hanamel, the prophet's cousin from Anathoth, appears miraculously in the midst of siege warfare to offer Jeremiah the right of redemption on land. The variety of characters along with Jeremiah's changing relationship to them underscores how reversals confront the prophet with choices, and how these choices require action to set processes in motion that may lead to a hopeful outcome.

Third Jeremiah acted even though the purchase of land made no sense to him. This fundamental doubt of the prophet is explored in his extended prayer in vv. 16-25. Verses 24-25 read:

> See, the siege-ramps have been cast up against the city to take it, and the city, faced with sword, famine, and pestilence, has been given into the hands of the Chaldeans who are fighting against it. . . . Yet you, O Lord GOD, have said to me, "Buy the field for money and get witnesses."

The structure of Jeremiah 32 suggests that the prophet's purchase of land was illogical and that the prophet, himself, was not convinced of the wisdom of such an action. Yet this action, performed in doubt, embodies hope because it actually created the future that becomes the basis of divine reassurance in vv. 26-42.

The Response: *Psalm 91:1-6, 14-16*

Protection in the Sanctuary

Setting. Psalm 91 is best characterized as a liturgy, because it incorporates a variety of different forms of speech. It begins with an invitation or summons to confession in vv. 1-2, then switches in the next section, when the speaker teaches other worshipers about the protective power of God in vv. 3-13, and, finally, the psalm ends with a divine oracle in vv. 14-16.

Structure. The lectionary has narrowed the scope of the psalm to include the opening summons to confession in vv. 1-2, introductory verses from the teaching section in vv. 4-6, and the divine oracle in vv. 14-16.

Significance. The setting of the psalm is clearly the sanctuary. The imagery of abiding in the shadow of the Almighty (v. 2) and of finding refuge under his wings (v. 4) is language from the cult, where God was envisioned as enthroned with winged cherubim overhead. The opening invitation is striking and lends itself to liturgical use in a contemporary worship service. It begins with an inclusive "You" but is then immediately qualified by two relative clauses, each of which begins with the word, *who.* Those being addressed are the ones who already live under the protection of God, and they are instructed to confess the fact in v. 2: "[You] will say to the LORD, 'my refuge and my fortress; my God, in whom I trust.' " The confession prompts preaching o⟶ ⟶ching in vv. 9-13, most likely by a worship leader. Note the c⟶ ⟶ sentence in v. 9: "Because you have made the LORD your ret⟶ . ." The teaching goes on to underscore how God will in fact⟶ ⟶ct those who put their trust in him. Then, the psalm actually ends with direct theophany in vv. 14-16, when God confirms the teaching of the worship leader. The language of trust provides important commentary on hope.

New Testament Texts

The epistle reading is parenetic material and the Gospel lesson is a parable, but the themes of wealth and proper regard for material goods is at the heart of both texts. Both I Timothy and Luke clearly recognize that one's life-style and commitment to God are related intricately to each other.

The Epistle: *I Timothy 6:6-19*

The Benefit of Piety That Brings Satisfaction

Setting. I Timothy moves toward its end with a final series of observations that criticize false teachers (6:2*b*-10), give advice on an active life of faithfulness (11-16), impart instructions for wealthy believers (17-19), and issue a closing charge and blessing (20-21). Our reading begins with v. 6 which is a new turn in the line of thought in vv. 2*b*-10. The reading continues through the final sections of the letter, stopping short of the seemingly personal words in vv. 20-21. The materials in this reading combine prosaic and poetic lines, which is evident from the way the Greek text is often set in modern scholarly versions of the New Testament. At times the language of the reading is not only poetic but also creedal in character. Thus many scholars conclude that the letter incorporates early Christian confessional materials into these verses.

Structure. Commentators recognize seven related sections in our reading. It is helpful in moving toward proclamation to follow the logic and the themes of the verses:

1. The recognizable value of piety that is characterized by contentment (v. 6);
2. The reasons why piety should bring contentment (vv. 7-8);
3. The dangers of piety that is not content but that looks for profits and wealth (vv. 9-10);
4. A call to disciplined living that looks to the future as it recalls the past (vv. 11-12);
5. An eschatological charge to Christ-like faithfulness (vv. 13-14);
6. A theological meditation and doxological declaration about the future appearance of Jesus Christ (vv. 15-16); and
7. A final word for wealthy Christians (vv. 17-19).

The logic from v. 6 through v. 16 spirals but is progressive and, while ideas come and go, they are related. Verses 17-19 seem to be an afterthought. Having warned against seeking wealth and having spoken of the riches of faith, the author offers concrete advice for persons who are already actually wealthy in material possessions.

Significance. The central theme of this reading is that there is great gain (or benefit) in godliness (or piety) with genuine attendant contentment (or satisfaction). While this theme is articulated here in a Christian writing, the idea of "contentment" would have been intelligible to a wide range of ancient readers. The Greek word translated as "contentment" is *autarkeia,* a word that occurs in the philosophical reflections of both Stoic and Cynic thinkers of the Hellenistic age. In such ancient philosophy the concept of "contentment" meant a sense of self-sufficiency, but that meaning is clearly not the point of this line in I Timothy. Rather, here the author battles against false teachers who pursue piety as a path to power, position, privilege, and prestige. These false teachers labor to be self-sufficient in the philosophers' sense of the term, and according to I Timothy that is their problem. They look to themselves and their own devices rather than to God and Christ as the sources of strength and direction in life. By speaking in one line of the "gain" of "godliness" with "contentment," I Timothy recognizes the satisfaction that comes with God-centered devotion. God as the ground of gratification is the goal of Christian life.

The poetic reflection in vv. 7-8 explains why the gain of godliness produces contentment. First, from the perspective of eschatological reality we learn the obvious truth that the riches accumulated in this life do not transfer to God's promised future. God, not goods, determine our future, and recognizing God's superiority should help free us from an inappropriate assessment of possessions. Second, the God-granted necessities of life are all we really need for existence as God intends it, and in relation to God's purposes we find our security and freedom. Even people who have merely been on vacation know the joy and freedom that comes from leaving most of what they own behind. 'Tis indeed a gift to be simple.

Verses 9-10 strike a negative note. The warning is not against wealth per se. The author does not say that money or possessions are inherently bad or that they necessarily corrupt. Rather, the desire, love, and craving for riches distorts one's perspective, life, and relationship to God.

The next section, vv. 11-12, calls Timothy away from such longings for wealth to a robust life in service to God's will. Timothy is named "God's man" in recognition of God's claim on his life. Then, v. 11 names God's values to which a believer is to be committed. The athletic metaphor of v. 12 urges Timothy to exercise the reality of faith, established in his original confession and aimed at the promise of eternal life.

The urgent appeals in vv. 11-12 are given an explicit theological and christological basis in vv. 13-14. The author refers to God the gracious Creator and to Christ Jesus whose own Passion established the norm of life to which Timothy (and all Christians) is called. Again, the eschatological nature of Christian life is recognized in the mention of the future appearance of the Lord Jesus Christ. In turn, in vv. 15-16 the author ventures into doxological recognition of God's sovereignty.

The final verses of the reading, vv. 17-19, are clear. The specific instructions for well-to-do Christians are consistent with all that has been written so far. The heart of the teaching centers on God's goodness and generosity. Because God is who he is, we set our hopes on him, and we live good and generous lives that reflect the reality of our relation to God, a reality that draws us forward into God's own future.

The Gospel: *Luke 16:19-31*

The Rich Man and Lazarus or the Story of Two Gulfs

Setting. As Jesus taught his disciples about the necessity of shrewdness in an uncompromising commitment to God, the Pharisees overheard his teachings about the impossibility of serving God and mammon. Luke tells his readers in 16:14 that the Pharisees were "lovers of money"; and so they scoffed at Jesus' teaching. In sharp response to the Pharisees' reaction Jesus makes a series of statements designed to show the true nature of human life from God's own point-of-view. The fourth and final item in Jesus' counter-teaching is the well-known and elaborate parable of the rich man and Lazarus.

Structure. The parable unfolds as a well-told story. The account is clear and coherent, although there are two major parts to the story: vv. 19-26 and vv. 27-31. In the first major section of the story there are two scenes that are connected by a narrative report. Initially vv. 19-21 establish a "this-worldly" contrast between the life of luxury of the rich man and the dire poverty of Lazarus; strikingly the gap exists despite the physical proximity in which these two characters live. A turn comes as v. 22 reports the death and fate of both Lazarus and the rich man. Then, in vv. 23-26 a second scene focuses on the "afterlife" where a great reversal of the fortunes of the rich man and Lazarus has occurred. Now, a great gulf separates the rich man and Lazarus.

In the second major part of the parable we learn of the rich man's appeal for Abraham to send Lazarus back into the world to warn the man's five brothers of the future peril they face in living lives of luxury indifferent to those who suffer. The conversation contains terms and phrases with crucial theological language and significance.

Significance. Jesus returned from the dead. Before his death and resurrection there were some who believed in him and who followed him, but many were indifferent. When Jesus was raised there is little evidence that things changed very much. Some believers saw him, and they were given necessary courage by their encounter with their risen Lord, but the majority of those who rejected Jesus prior to his crucifixion still refused to recognize this person and his work after his resurrection. Abraham's final statement to the poor rich man in v. 31 tells the truth about the world's reaction to Jesus Christ.

The other dimension of Abraham's statement that demands attention is his mention of the value of Moses (the Pentateuch) and the prophets (the Old Testament books by and about the prophets of Israel). Abraham tells the rich man that God had long been at work in Israel to declare and to establish God's own standards for human life. The God who acted in Jesus Christ acted, according to Christian faith, definitively and ultimately; but this christo-centric act was consistent with what God had been doing among the people of Israel through the ages. Thus, the sorry state of human relations—great and indifferent wealth over against great and debilitating poverty— is not in accordance with God's perennially revealed will and work.

The original gap between the rich man and Lazarus was a purely human construction. The rich man ignored poor Lazarus at his gate. We should notice when the rich man speaks to Abraham that he even knows Lazarus's name. Perhaps we are to understand that in his life of luxury this man could name real suffering, but he kept himself aloof from the pain of poverty as he led a life of opulent self-gratification. In turn, contrast the second gap, now a great, wide, fixed chasm that no one can cross. This gulf is no human product; it exists as a result of God's final judgment. Here we not only see God's will, but, as in God's raising the once-dead Jesus, we see God's ultimate authority finally to establish the will and the ways that God has been laboring to bring into being throughout human history.

This parable confronts and threatens affluent and indifferent Christians. Whatever we gain we have by the grace of God. As we see the world around us, it is possible—even as we affirm Moses, the prophets, and the resurrection of Jesus Christ—to go on living selfishly in a manner that God ultimately condemns. We must ask ourselves whether we shall go on living according to our own wishes, attending to our every desire, or whether we shall reform our lives so as to live according to God's revealed and stated will.

Proper 21: The Celebration

Fall is the usual time in most churches for the Every-Member Canvass, Stewardship Sunday, or whatever the event is called that is designed to meet the budget for the coming year. Today's lessons are admirably suited for such an occasion. Because we are in ordinary time and the lessons are being read sequentially, it will make little difference if these lessons are exchanged with those for the Sunday when the stewardship emphasis is made (excluding, of course, All Saints Sunday and Christ the King).

The lessons for today set the stage for a discussion by the worship committee of the reason all the liturgical revisions place the offering after the sermon. This has occasioned much controversy in local churches, and it has usually had little to do with the theological model that the order of worship is intended to represent. The assertion that the post-sermon offering seems like a comment on the value of the sermon only serves to underscore a misplaced emphasis on the sermon as the most important component of the Sunday service. And it is no help to counter-assert that the offering before the sermon has the appearance of paying an entrance fee. In both cases the essential theological argument has been missed. Consider that the offering is a response to hearing God's Word, which gives us direction for the ordering of our lives. Jeremiah makes an investment in the future at God's direction and out of faith in God's plans, not because he thought it was a good idea or simply because he wanted "to make a statement." Jesus condemns Dives because he did not learn from God's word (Moses and the prophets) how he should respond in compassion to others. The writer to Timothy obviously feels that the reception of Christ into one's life has consequences for how we use our resources. The offering, in other words, is consequent upon our hearing the Word and is symbolic of our faithful response.

One or two other observations about the receiving of the offering in public worship may be made. If prayer is offered, then the prayer should dedicate the gifts after they have been received rather than exhort the congregation beforehand to greater generosity in some oblique fashion. No more prayer over empty plates, unless our intent is to manipulate! And, while we are still squirming, is it possible that some sung response other than the Doxology might be more appropriate from time to time? Except for its line "from whom all blessings flow," what makes the Doxology particularly relevant to the presentation of the offering anyway? And do we wish to equate money with "all blessings"? What other resources does your hymnal have for the presentation of offerings? If there is a sung response, is a prayer necessary?

The hymn, "Fight the Good Fight," is based on II Timothy 6:12.

Proper Twenty-two Sunday Between October 2 and 8 Inclusive

Old Testament Texts

Lamentations 1:1-6 and Psalm 137 mourn the destruction of Jerusalem.

The Lesson: *Lamentations 1:1-6*

A Funeral Dirge over Zion

Setting. The book of Lamentations is made up of five poems that separate into five chapters. The first four poems are acrostic in structure. The subject matter of the book consists of laments over the fall of Jerusalem in 587 B.C.E.

Structure. Lamentations 1:1-6 does not separate into any clear divisions beyond the acrostic structure. Verses 1-6 comprise the first six letters of the Hebrew alphabet (*aleph, bet, gimmel, dalet, he, waw*).

Significance. Lamentations 1:1-6 describes in vivid detail the fact of the exile by personifying Zion in a poem that suggests a funeral dirge. The poem opens in v. 1 with an exclamation or a wail, "Oh how!" This cry gives way to three contrasts. Jerusalem, which was once full of people, great among the nations, and a princess among provinces now stands alone, like a widow or a vassal. As a result of this situation the city is personified in the v. 2 as weeping. The reasons for lamentation are provided again through contrast. Instead of comfort from lovers, Jerusalem receives treachery from enemies. The lamentation is finally given historical specificity in v. 3. It is because of the exile that Zion mourns. Personification and contrast continue throughout the remainder of vv. 4-6: the roads to Zion mourn because no one travels them for festivals, princes now lack strength, and the enemies of Zion prosper. Verse 5 provides a theological reason by making reference to past transgressions in Zion and God's punishment. Beyond this reference, however, Lamentation 1:1-6 provides a stark image of the fact of the exile rather than its theological consequences.

The Response: *Psalm 137*

A Lament over the Loss of Zion

Setting. Psalm 137 stands out because of the historically specific references to Babylon and to the exile. The precise details of rivers, willow trees, the hanging up of harps on branches, captors, and the request for national songs has prompted scholars to classify the psalm as a ballad. Others have questioned such a designation by suggesting that the precise details in the psalm are a description of recurring liturgical actions performed in conjunction with an observance of lamenting. In either case, it is clear that Psalm 137 is a lament about loss, and, as such, it is an appropriate response to Lamentations 1:1-6. If Lamentations 1:1-6 described the fact of the exile through its series of contrasts in which Zion was personified, then Psalm 137 explores the repercussions of this event on the life of faith for exilic Israel.

Structure. Psalm 137 separates into three parts: a lament in vv. 1-4, in vv. 5-6 a voice emerges declaring unending loyalty to Zion, and imprecations against the destroyers of Zion in vv. 7-9.

Significance. When using this psalm in worship, the leader should determine what is the loss that is worthy of lament. What does it mean to lose Zion? And why is it that Songs of Zion cannot be sung in a foreign land?

First, the loss of Zion is not a psychological problem. The psalm is not primarily about being sad, even though images or communal weeping are prominent. Furthermore, the loss of Zion is not about nostalgia—the good old days. Nor is the lament about the hardship of exilic life. All of these aspects of the psalm are certainly true to the experience of the exiles, but they do not go to the root problem of the psalm. Rather than a psychological term, *Zion* is a cosmological term (see the discussion below). When this psalm is read psychologically, we are very uncomfortable with the imprecations at the end in v. 9. It is one thing to be sad, but is it really necessary to smash in the skulls of babies? Dropping the verse is a dishonest way to "fix" the problem.

Second, the loss of Zion is a collapse of a whole world view that gave meaning to theological discourse and direction to the life of faith for ancient Israel. The destruction of the Temple and the loss of the land provided a direct challenge to Israel's faith. They believed, after all, that their God was the all-powerful, universal king, who gave them the land of Canaan as the gift of salvation, and guaranteed this gift for all time by literally living in the Temple in Jerusalem. The word *Zion* was meant to symbolize each of these aspects of Israel's faith, and the fact of the exile called the truth of the whole belief system into question. With the destruction of Jerusalem and the Temple, as well as the loss of the land, what had been a central structure to provide meaning and direction for the life of faith (Zion) was subsumed into the much larger social and religious system of Babylon. In the process, Zion was reduced to interesting folklore at the fringes of a new and bigger society. Verse 3 illustrates this point. Here, the Babylonians, who have brought different ethnic groups into the capitol from the four corners of the earth, ask the Judeans to sing some of their tribal religious songs, "Sing us one of the songs of Zion!" The problem for the psalmist is that Zion is not simply interesting folklore meant to enrich someone else's life with cultural diversity; Zion's song is a confession about the foundation of all meaning in the world. The request, therefore, is a challenge to the very truth of Zion. Verses 7-9 underscore this point by lifting Babylon to mythological proportions, where it is pictured as a demonic devastator seeking to remove the very foundations of reality. If Zion is true, then Babylon must be its destroyer.

Psalm 137 represents the voice of faith when there appears to be no evidence for belief. This voice does not provide easy theological conclusions, but is resolute in a commitment to continue journeying with God. How do you sing a song of Zion when the traditional language of faith is no longer meaningful? In such situations, the very act of lamenting is a statement of faith. A mourner complains bitterly to a God who is absent or hidden, but not to a God who is extinct.

New Testament Texts

The epistle is a slightly nostalgic appeal to give one's life to the transforming power of the Spirit, so that the power of the Spirit may employ one's life in service to the will of God as known through Jesus Christ. The lesson from Luke takes up the matters of faith and service, treating the themes of the power of faith and the character of Christian service.

The Epistle: *II Timothy 1:1-14*

The Spirit Working in You and Through You

Setting. Second Timothy is known, along with I Timothy and Titus, as one of the Pastoral Epistles. Scholars debate the authorship of this writing (and the other two letters), but they have employed this designation for over 250 years, because these three letters depict a pastor, Paul, writing to other pastors, Timothy and Titus, about genuinely pastoral concerns. The situations in which these letters portray Paul are different from one letter to the other. In II Timothy Paul is in prison in Rome, and Timothy seems to be in Ephesus (clearly his location according to I Timothy). Paul has had one hearing concerning certain charges against him, and that audience went well despite real adversity. Yet, at the time of the writing of II Timothy the apostle foresees his death. Thus, he writes to Timothy to warn him about problems and to advise him about building up the church. Ultimately, Paul calls for Timothy to come to him, and he asks Timothy to bring specific items to him in prison. Nevertheless, II Timothy is primarily concerned with false teaching and sound doctrine.

Structure. The verses of the reading come from three distinct portions of the epistle. First, vv. 1-2 are the opening or salutation of the letter. Second, vv. 3-5 are the letter's thanksgiving. Third, vv. 6-14 are the initial paragraph of the body of the letter; in fact, they are the initial lines of the first major section of the body of the letter which runs from 1:6 through 2:13 and makes an appeal for Spirit-inspired faithfulness despite the humiliation of Christian suffering. Thus, a sermon on these verses could treat the related general themes of greetings, thanksgiving, and appeal—although for the sermon to be germane to this reading one will need to attend to the particular manner in which the verses of the lesson develop these general themes.

Significance. In the verses of this reading one encounters much of the quasi-technical vocabulary of early Christian faith and practice. The verses also weave together theological convictions and personal reflections. For preaching today the theological dimensions of the passage are more important than the personal remarks, although at times Paul and Timothy are more embodiments of the theology of the verses than mere individuals. A sermon could easily reflect upon Paul and Timothy as illustrations of the theological dimensions of the text; indeed, putting flesh on the theology of the text may help apply the theology to the real flesh-and-blood persons who make up the Church in the world today.

The salutation recognizes the superiority or supremacy of God's will and the commission to ministry by Christ Jesus. As an apostle, literally "one sent out" in service, Paul does God's will, and that work brings him into divinely altered relations to other humans. For example, now we find that Timothy is Paul's "beloved child," although there was certainly no blood relations between these two men. Rather, Timothy became Paul's child according to the will of God in Jesus Christ. The life of Christ, given in suffering for the accomplishment of God's salvation of humanity and raised up to abolish death, has instilled new life in both Paul and Timothy, so that they are related to each other through Christ in a bond that can be described only by the intimate and powerful metaphor of family—of father and son.

As the powerful Spirit of God at work in and through Christ Jesus grasped Paul and altered his very existence from opponent to advocate of Jesus Christ, so the same Spirit reaches through the inspired ministry of Paul and grasps others—namely, Timothy. This letter recalls the transforming work of the Spirit in such a way that Timothy is both reminded of his experience of saving grace and called to give himself whole-heartedly to the work of the indwelling Spirit, so that the same work of Spirit-transformation that Timothy knew may continue to reach out through Timothy to still others.

Furthermore, the verses of this reading recognize the reality that Christ Jesus himself and, in turn, his followers suffer as they do God's will. The power of the Spirit is no guarantee of comfort, although the Spirit inspires a boldness and love in the lives of Christians that keeps them secure despite the worst forms of hostility. Timothy hears of Paul's confidence in the Lord, and the letter appeals to him (Timothy) to embody the same absolute trust in God. The letter emphasizes the urgency of this appeal by employing the phrase "until that day" in v. 12. The language of this line imparts an earnest eschatological tone to the statements, and in preaching from this reading one will do well to give the sermon a similar sense of boldness and urgency.

The Gospel: *Luke 17:5-10*

Transforming Faith and Unassuming Service

Setting. In relation to the lesson for Proper Eighteen we noted that Luke's account of Jesus' journey to Jerusalem (9:51–19:27) unfolds in three major sections (9:51–13:21; 13:22–17:10; 17:11–19:27). The lesson for this Sunday comes at the very end of the second major section, which treats predominantly the theme of the deliverance of the lost. In reaction to Jesus' warnings and admonitions in 17:1-4, Luke tells us that the apostles asked Jesus to increase their faith. Jesus responded to this request, so that we find Jesus teaching the apostles in metaphorical language about the power of faith (vv. 5-6) and, then, continuing to speak about the appropriate attitude for faithful service (vv. 7-10). The second portion of the lesson, the parable of the dutiful servant, is a tradition found only in Luke; while the first teaching about faith the size of a mustard seed is strikingly similar to Matthew 17:19-20, although the versions of the saying are sufficiently distinct to allow us through comparison to perceive each evangelist's emphases.

Structure. At a glance the lesson seems to have two unrelated parts, vv. 5-6, the metaphorical or parabolic exchange between the apostles and the Lord concerning the increasing of the apostles' faith, and vv. 7-10, the parable of the "unworthy" servant with its pointed instructions at the conclusion. Yet, the lectionary committee may have seen Luke's subtle purpose in placing these two originally independent traditions (compare Matthew who has a version of the first part but no trace of the second). At the outset of Luke 17 Jesus speaks of the danger of temptation to sin and the necessity of boundless forgiveness for those who repent. His teaching provokes the question concerning faith in v. 5; then, his answer follows in v. 6. Jesus speaks of faith, but he talks only of its power in v. 6. Verses 7-10 seem to "follow up" on the faith-talk by defining the proper attitude of those whose faith would result in powerful service. Thus, while some reflection is necessary to see the connection between vv. 5-6 and 7-10, the verses of the lesson are not haphazardly arranged. One may choose to preach from only one part or the other of the lesson, although a challenge for creative proclamation lies in the lesson as a whole.

Significance. As Jesus begins to reply to the petition of the disciples, he speaks in hyperbolic images from horticulture that are clearly not to be taken literally. A five-year-old child who once heard a reading of Jesus' remarks said, "He didn't really mean that, he just said it that way to make it more interesting." With the stumbling block of literalism removed, we do have to ask ourselves what Jesus was talking about. His metaphorical statement communicates a great truth—namely, faith alters the essential nature of things. Jesus is talking about the dynamic change that occurs through faith. A tree by nature grows in the soil, but Jesus says a modicum of faith can so dramatically alter perceived reality that a tree can be planted in the sea. Faith can alter life itself, and faith is particularly powerful in its capacity to change patterns of relationships. Persons whose lives have been radically altered by the power of faith testify to the reality of faith's capacity to change. One person had a problem with honesty, another with trying to manipulate others; this person had no capacity to care, that one had the wrong set of priorities. Now they testify to the transformation of their lives by faith.

The changes wrought by the power of faith occur for a purpose. As God through Jesus Christ alters a human life through faith, the new life given to the person takes the form of a life of unassuming service. Because a person knows her or his life to be the result of the power of faith, there is no arrogance in the new life that one lives. Thus, Jesus continues to speak, talking beyond the immediate point of the disciples' request, to teach them about the character of a life of faithful service. The parable of the unworthy servant is a lesson about discipleship. We should not attempt to find images of God in the servant's master. The master seems more a despot than a person of grace and love. Rather, the parable aims at deflating false expectations about a life of Christian service. In a sense the service rendered in this parable is its own reward, for Jesus' concluding remark tells us that the faithful servants deem themselves "unworthy," for they have merely done what they were told to do as servants. Jesus' story teaches us a proper self-understanding in relation to the doing of God's will. We are to do that work to which God directs us without expectations of divine praise or thanks. Faith that leads to service does not foster great expectations for ourselves, for faith and the commission to service are themselves God's good gifts to us.

Proper 22: The Celebration

The Sunday of Proper Twenty-two will in most years be World Communion Sunday for many congregations, and preachers may well ask how three such diverse lessons as are appointed for today can be in any way related to that general theme. A starting point is to consider how the absence of God/Christ is a reality in both the Old Testament and the epistle lessons. God has departed from Zion, and the church is in a posture of waiting for "that Day" of the Lord's final appearing and triumph. In the Eucharist, however, the Christian community asserts that it is given an assurance of the on-going presence of Christ in its midst, and participation in the meal itself is a foretaste of heaven. Charles Wesley called it an "antepast of heaven." It has the same root as *antipasto,* which we eat before the main course. The Gospel reading suggests that this presence of Christ, this anticipation of the reign of God in the sacred meal, is one of the results of faithful service.

The belief is widespread that acts of prayer and the doing of good works only have value if we "feel like it." We make our feelings paramount and deny that God is able to work positively upon us in spite of them. We idolize our feelings, and we have lost any understanding of public worship as something done rather than something experienced. The Caroline divine, Lancelot Andrewes, said that if our worship is only inward, "with our hearts and not our hats," something necessary is lacking. This loss of the liturgical sense results in making public worship seem like one-half of a conversation in which the other speaker is entirely silent. The church celebration of World Communion Sunday today is an effort to worship with our hats, to find God and Christ in tangible things, to be faithful to the Lord's command to keep the feast until he comes.

II Timothy 1:6 is reflected in the last line of the third stanza of Wesley's hymn, "O Thou Who Camest from Above." The entire hymn will fit well today as a bridge between the epistle and Gospel readings.

> 1. O Thou who camest from above
> the pure celestial fire to impart,
> kindle a flame of sacred love
> on the mean altar of my heart.
>
> 2. There let it for thy glory burn
> with inextinguishable blaze,
> and trembling to its source return
> in humble prayer and fervent praise.
>
> 3. Jesus, confirm my heart's desire
> to work, and speak, and think for thee;
> still let me guard the holy fire,
> and still stir up thy gift in me.
>
> 4. Ready for all thy perfect will,
> my acts of faith and love repeat,
> till death thy endless mercies seal,
> and make the sacrifice complete.

The hymn appears to the tune "Hereford" in *The United Methodist Hymnal* (No. 501) and the Episcopal *The Hymnal* 1982 (no. 704). The Episcopalians seem unwilling to refer to the "mean" altar of the heart, however, and so lose a point of contact with the Gospel reading! The tune "Germany" is also suggested for use with the hymn.

Proper Twenty-three Sunday Between October 9 and 15 Inclusive

Old Testament Texts

Jeremiah 29:1, 4-7 is the account of a letter that Jeremiah sent to the exiles in Babylon. Psalm 66:1-12 is a hymn of praise.

The Lesson: *Jeremiah 29:1, 4-7*

When Orthodoxy Becomes the Lie

Setting. R.P. Carroll, in his commentary on *Jeremiah* (Old Testament Library [Philadelphia: Westminster, 1986]) suggests that Jeremiah 27–29 is an independent unit within the larger book of Jeremiah. The setting and time of these chapters is similar: Jerusalem at the "beginning of the reign of King Zedekiah" (27:1 and also 28:1), which is the date of the first exile in 597 B.C.E. Note how the spelling of Jeremiah (*yirmeyahu* versus *yirmeyah*), Zedekiah (*sideqiyyah* versus *sideqiyyah*), and Nebuchadnezzar (versus *Nebuchadrezzar*) are different in these chapters as compared to their use in the remainder of the book. Furthermore the chapters are organized around the same problem: The defeat of Jerusalem, the exile of its ruling elite, and how these events were to be interpreted theologically. The central theological question was whether God was abandoning Jerusalem or simply testing the people through a momentary crisis. As one might guess, voices arise on both sides of this debate, which gave rise to the problem of who was right, especially when both sides claimed to speak for God. Jeremiah 27–29 explores the problem of true and false prophecy within the setting of the crisis in 597 B.C.E.

The force of the theological problem requires a brief review of the historical circumstances of the first deportation in Jerusalem. In 597 B.C.E. Nebuchadnezzar defeated Jerusalem, causing King Jehoiachin to surrender, which resulted in the first deportation consisting of the king as well as leading citizens, and the plundering of the royal and Temple treasures. The loss of a king and the ruling elite is a serious social problem, but the sack of the Temple was a religious problem and not simply a social or national problem. At the heart of the Judean faith was the confession that God dwelt in the Temple and that the divine presence was permanent. This meant that Jerusalem and the Temple were secure from invasion because a divine promise was much stronger than any foreign army. Psalm 48 celebrates this fundamental belief. It begins with praise:

> Great is the LORD and greatly to be praised
>   in the city of our God
> ....
> Mount Zion, in the far north,
>   the city of the great King.
> Within its citadels God has shown himself a sure defense.

Because of God's presence in Jerusalem, invasion was not an acceptable possibility. The psalm continues:

> Then the kings assembled,
>   they came on together.
> As soon as they saw it, they were astounded;
>   they were in panic, they took to flight.

After this ritual defeat of the nations the psalmist breaks in, now as a worshiper within the Temple:

> As we have heard, so have we seen
>   in the city of the LORD of hosts,
> in the city of our God, which God establishes forever.

Jeremiah 27–29 is a circumstantial debate about the truth of Psalm 48 in the year 597 B.C.E.

Structure. Jeremiah's letter to the exiles in 29:1, 4-7 occurs at the close of the cycle in chapters 27–29. An overview of this larger unit will provide context for interpreting the function of the letter within

71

the larger conflict over true and false prophecy. Jeremiah 27 begins with the prophet Jeremiah putting a yoke on his shoulders as a symbolic action that the Babylonian conquest was not simply a momentary problem but a far more permanent situation. The prophet's actions are in conflict with a majority opinion that stressed how God would quickly reverse this situation. Chapter 28 gives the majority opinion a voice in the person of Hananiah, who breaks Jeremiah's yoke and states that God would quickly do the same to the Babylonian, which leads to a confrontation between the two prophets. Jeremiah warns Israel not to trust in the lie that Hananiah was perpetuating. This conflict continues into chapter 29 when Jeremiah writes to the exiles (those in the first deportation of 597 B.C.E.) and advises them to settle in for the long haul. Jeremiah's letter creates a conflict with a letter from a prophet named Shemaiah, who wrote just the opposite to the exiles—namely that they should prepare to return.

Significance. Who is a true prophet? Who is false? This is a very difficult issue for the preacher because both preacher and congregation identify immediately with Jeremiah. It is his words, after all, that are canonized. He most certainly is the true prophet, but this conclusion overlooks a central tension in this text when it is read in the setting of the Israelite monarchy: Jeremiah's "true words" are heresy in the year 597 B.C.E., and it is the conclusion of his opponents that reflects biblical orthodoxy. Psalm 48 supports Hananiah and Shemaiah and not Jeremiah. Furthermore, given the circumstances of the situation, Hananaiah and Shemaiah have taken the more difficult position. The city, after all, has been defeated. To proclaim the power of God in the midst of such overwhelmingly contradictory evidence appears to be the stronger act of faith and indeed it is supported by tradition. Yet they are wrong. In the year 597 B.C.E. a simple reaffirmation of tradition is a lie, and its denial is true prophecy. Do we dare preach that Jeremiah is the true prophet precisely because he has rejected orthodoxy?

Jeremiah 27–29 is a strong message about God and change. It presents a warning of how the mere preservation of tradition, especially when it is out of strong religious convictions, can itself through time become a lie. Jeremiah 27–29 is not constructed to be preached in all times and places. It has been placed carefully by editors in the setting of 597 B.C.E. Perhaps the goal of the preacher is to find the equivalent of the conflict between Jeremiah and the prophets in the year 597 B.C.E. within the contemporary congregation. Where has orthodoxy become a lie in the life of your church? Jeremiah is the voice that calls such beliefs into question. Such lies can be subtle, which makes them all the more powerful. Even the boundaries of the lectionary verses illustrate how lies can work their way into our religious life. Note how the very limited boundaries of Jeremiah 29:1, 4-7 turn Jeremiah's letter to the exiles into something else altogether, by eliminating the larger conflict of true and false prophecy in which the letter was meant to function. The central point of Jeremiah's letter is not the well being of the exiles or the Babylonians, as a reading of vv. 1, 4-7 in isolation would lead the interpreter to conclude (especially when it is accompanied with a hymn of praise in Psalm 66:1-12). Rather the text of the letter points to a critique of orthodox comfort. In view of this the preacher may wish to include the contrasting letter by Shemaiah (vv. 24-28) and the divine response to it (vv. 29-32) with the lectionary reading.

The Response: *Psalm 66:1-12*

A Hymn

Setting. Psalm 66 is composed of two separate compositions. Verses 1-12 are categorized as a hymn of praise, in which God's acts of salvation are celebrated. Verses 13-20 shift the focus to an individual psalm of thanksgiving, where God's constancy to answer prayer is confessed.

Structure. Psalm 66:1-12 separates into three sections. Verses 1-4 are a call to praise. The verses suggests some kind of choral response. Verses 1-2 represent a leader calling the worshipers to praise, while vv. 4-4 are the congregations response. Note the words in v. 3, "Say to God. . . ." Verses 5-7 provide reasons when God is worthy of praise. These verses recount the Exodus and Gods subsequent rule over the nations. Verses 8-12 shift into the mood of thanksgiving.

Significance. When Psalm 66:1-12 is read as a response to Jeremiah 27-29 the language of being tested in vv. 10-12 stands out.

Such testing may be a simplistic understanding of the Exodus that is recounted in vv. 5-7. If such a reading is followed, then the liturgist may wish to add the second half of the psalm, where God's constancy to answer prayer is confessed. Prayer has the power to break through to God, even when biblical orthodoxy stands between ourselves and God.

New Testament Texts

The epistle issues an admonition to faithfulness and the Gospel tells a story concerned with the nature of faith. The exhortation of the epistle presents statements that instruct us on the substance of faith and the Gospel story reflects upon the dynamics of faith. Both the epistle and the Gospel are concerned with the real-life outcomes or applications of faith.

The Epistle: *II Timothy 2:8-15*

"Remembering and Reminding"

Setting. Our epistle reading draws from the very personal, though theological, advice of the pastor to his younger colleague in ministry. At 2:1 the pastor sounds the theme of the larger section from which our reading comes—namely, "Be strong in the grace that is in Christ Jesus." The call of the pastor is to focused ministry that looks to God's work in Jesus Christ. Timothy is to remember Jesus Christ, and while remembering him, Timothy is to tell those among whom he labors of the meaning of faith in Christ Jesus.

Structure. The verses of our reading draw from two related sections of the letter. Verses 1-13 are an exhortation to endure suffering through the grace of Christ Jesus, and vv. 14-26 are a call to faithfulness in the face of heresy, that is, to faithfulness that may bring others to repentance. In our lesson, vv. 8-13 recall the foundations and the substance of Christian faith, seemingly recording an early Christian confession or creed in vv. 11-13. Then, vv. 14-15 exhort Timothy to active ministry that offers others both direction and an example for their own lives.

Significance. The opening statement of our lesson, "Remember

Jesus Christ," identifies the heart of Christian faith and practice. The manner in which the pastor writes is instructive for us as Christians today. Specifically, in remembering Jesus Christ, Timothy is told to recognize the power of God that was revealed in God's raising the crucified Jesus from the dead. Moreover, in mentioning Jesus' Davidic descent, the pastor reminds Timothy that recalling the power and glory of the resurrection does not mean that we lose sight of Jesus' true humanity. Too often today we attempt to do Christian theology as an abstraction. The person and work of Jesus are even less than the "presupposition of Christian theology" that some have regarded them. Christian faith can never forget Jesus and God's work through him. When there is no remembering of Jesus, there will be no clear, concrete understanding of God, God's will, and God's work. Christianity without Jesus Christ is not Christianity.

Indeed, the reality of Jesus Christ and God's work through him is an actuality that merits or demands our loyalty. Timothy is called to devotion to Jesus Christ that remains faithful even to the point of suffering. Strikingly, the pastor's words reveal that he understands that even in the suffering and oppression of faithful Christians the gospel is active in the world. Again, we should notice the focus of the faithfulness to which the pastor calls Timothy: Faithfulness is to Jesus Christ for the elect. Christ-centered living means service and benefits, not for ourselves, but for others.

In v. 10 and the creedal lines of vv. 11-12 we see further that while Christian faith has historical foundations in relation to Jesus Christ, Christian faith also has an eternal hope in relation to the promise of resurrection. Faithfulness to Jesus Christ may require suffering here and now, but it also promises glory in the future. Is this belief the delusion of "pie in the sky by and by"? It may have that appearance to persons who do not share the certitude afforded those committed to Jesus Christ, but to people of faith the hope of God-given glory, despite present oppression, is a vital reality that energizes steadfast living.

The lines of the creed examine present Christian experience and hope. Christians live transformed lives. They live knowing there is even more and greater transformation to come. Christians know their Lord has called them to steadfastness despite adversities, but they also know that their Lord is at work to achieve the promise of a different future. Indeed, the warning against faithlessness recognizes that the Lord's work is being done in this life in a very real way through the faithfulness of believers. Yet, the closing line of the confession recognizes beyond doubt that Christ is the focus and the source of Christian existence. Steadfast believers do not simply themselves bring about the glory of God's future, for Christ himself is faithful, even when we are faithless; and he pursues his own ends even when our efforts fail. The good news is that the hope of the future does not purely rest with us, although we are certainly called to current service. The gospel is the good news that transformation, hope, and steadfastness are ultimately founded in Christ himself.

Finally, vv. 14-15 direct Timothy to action. He is to live out his faith in Christ Jesus toward others. As the pastor called Timothy to steadfastness and faithfulness, so Timothy is to do the same in relation to others. In such activity, Timothy becomes an example to others of the truth of the gospel. Thus, we learn that the outcome of our faithfulness has crucial meaning for others; it is not simply an accomplishment for ourselves.

The Gospel: *Luke 17:11-19*

True Faith

Setting. Since Luke 9:51 we have known that Jesus was on the way to Jerusalem. Once again Luke reminds the readers of his account of Jesus ministry of Jesus' destination. In part, the note in v. 11 about Jesus' goal is necessary, since Jesus has been slow to reach his destination; but, at the same time, the mention of Jesus' being on the way to Jerusalem always reminds us of the fate that awaited Jesus in the Holy City. The Jesus who encountered the ten lepers somewhere between Samaria and Galilee is the same Jesus who suffered and died an ignoble death on the cross. Jesus himself knew suffering and rejection, so that the compassion shown to the lepers came from standing in solidarity with them in the real pain of life.

Structure. Luke tells this memorable story in an economical and deliberate style. All preachers should hope to make such a lasting impression with so few words. First, Luke sets the story geographically (v. 11). Then, he introduces the lepers with their clear problem and reports their effective appeal for mercy (vv. 12-13). In response, Jesus gives directions that the lepers follow (v. 14). Then, the story takes a striking turn as the one leper finds himself healed and turns back to Jesus (vv. 15-16). At the sight of the leper Jesus asks two more-than-rhetorical questions (vv. 17-18). Then, Jesus pronounces a benediction on the leper that gives a new twist to the course of events (v. 19). In reading the account carefully, human need, divine response, obedience, gratitude, the nature of faith, and freedom are revealed as the major themes of this lesson.

Significance. On his way to suffer and die in obedient compliance with God's willful work for the salvation of all humanity, Jesus was met by ten lepers. The plight of these people is not immediately clear to modern readers of this story, so that some consideration of the social situation of the lepers is helpful. In the world in which these people lived, they were considered unclean. The general reaction to a leper was similar to the unfortunate, but common, reaction to people with AIDS today. According to religious law, especially Leviticus 13–14, lepers were to wear torn garments, cover their mouths, and cry out, "Unclean," whenever they were in the vicinity of others. They could not live among healthy persons, so the only community available to them was with other lepers. The degree of their shame and the way it cast them beyond the boundaries of normal society is implicit in the details of this story. Here we find ten lepers, and at least one of the group was a Samaritan. Normally Jews and Samaritans had nothing to do with one another, but here the condition of leprosy made old distinctions and hostilities irrelevant. The lepers were united in their disgrace and pain.

The lepers go to Jesus. In their pain they cry out to him (as, through history, many other people have), and he hears them (as he has, through the ages, heard the painful cry of others). Forming historical analogies to illustrate both the painful cry of the lepers and the gracious response of Jesus Christ may help members of the congregation "identify" with this story. The preacher need not simply think about leprosy, for the pain of other diseases, accidents, deaths, and broken marriages have all driven people to call out to Jesus Christ for mercy.

Notice Jesus' reply. He issues a commandment. A commandment had made these people unacceptable to society, and now by means of a commandment Jesus directs these persons back into the mainstream of life. Luke tells us that the lepers obeyed. We do not find them hesitating or objecting to the directions. We simply learn that they went to show themselves to the priests so that they could be pronounced clean, and so, fit for normal human life. In the obedience of these lepers we see a kind of faith.

Yet, the story continues with the one Samaritan leper finding himself healed and, then, promptly returning and bowing down before Jesus and giving thanks. Here is true worship, and here indeed is true faith. This leper goes beyond the obedience of his comrades and manifests the joyful, reverent gratitude that characterizes a fully-formed faith. As the Samaritan acts out the depths of his faith, Jesus' questions show that the experience of grace leads to the praise of God for persons of mature faith. Indeed, the strange final pronouncement by Jesus clearly recognizes the dynamics of true faith. Because most translations read as does the NRSV, "Get up and go on your way; your faith has made you well," it is easy to misunderstand that mustering enough faith is the key to experiencing God's grace. Nothing could be further from the truth. The line may also be translated, "Your faith has made you whole." A truly whole human relates to God's will in more than mere obedience, although obedience is the beginning of faith. A truly whole person has a faith characterized by joy, reverence, and praise as well as obedience. And, as Jesus' statement—"Get up and go on your way"—recognizes, fully-formed faith brings a new freedom that gives one a relationship to God that goes beyond the dynamics of commandment-and-obedience.

Proper 23: The Celebration

We live in a time of heated religious controversy, and theological questions are at the heart of many of the ethical and moral issues being debated—abortion, euthanasia, human sexuality, and genetic engineering. The come-let-us-reason-together approach doesn't seem to have much chance against the thus-says-the-Lord attitude. If one is truly committed to a particular theological stance, what sense does it make to work out a compromise with another opinion? Isn't that a betrayal of God and the truth? Both the expanded Old Testament lesson (see commentary above) and the epistle lesson (continue reading through v. 18) raise for us the "good prophet, bad prophet" conundrum. This is nothing new for Christianity. In the sixteenth century such polarities precipitated the religious wars that devastated Europe and discredited Christianity for large numbers of people who could not reconcile wholesale slaughter in the name of the Prince of Peace.

Orthodoxy, it would appear, is not as easy to determine as we would like. Indeed, it is often from the perspective of historical distance that we are able to make any decisions about who may have been right. The Gospel lesson suggests that faith is more than belief, more than adherence to a list of dogmatic formulations. The Samaritan had already been healed before he returned to give thanks, but it was only then that Jesus told him that his faith had made him whole (see commentary). He had been healed by his faithful obedience to Jesus' command, but his act of thanksgiving had made him whole. It may be instructive to note here that the Creed was among the latest arrivals in the liturgy because when the Great Thanksgiving was prayed the faith of the church was being declared. Creeds only became necessary as the eucharistic prayer became more removed from the people. What place does thanksgiving have in our process of defining God or doing theology? Does the word *joys* in "Joys and Concerns" tend to trivialize what should be encompassed by *thanksgiving?* How might an attitude of thanksgiving "for our creation, preservation, and all the blessings of this life" inform any discussion about abortion or euthanasia? Can the false prophet survive long in an environment of thanksgiving?

The new services in many churches are designed to move from the proclamation of the Word to the eucharistic order, to the Great Thanksgiving of the church. On non-eucharistic occasions, most of the services suggest that the service conclude with a shorter prayer of thanksgiving, which will maintain the eucharistic emphasis. The General Thanksgiving of the *Book of Common Prayer* is one of the liturgical treasures of the English language, and should be used at least occasionally. Following is its rendition in more contemporary language. Notice how it moves us to consider the consequences of thanksgiving for Christian life.

> Almighty God, Father of all mercies,
> we your unworthy servants give you humble thanks
> for all your goodness and loving-kindness
> to us and to all whom you have made.
> We bless you for our creation, preservation,
> and all the blessings of this life;
> but above all for your immeasurable love
> in the redemption of the world by our Lord Jesus Christ;
> for the means of grace, and for the hope of glory.
> And, we pray, give us such an awareness of your mercies,
> that with truly thankful hearts we may show forth your praise,
> not only with our lips, but in our lives,
> by giving up our selves to your service,
> and by walking before you
> in holiness and righteousness all our days;
> through Jesus Christ our Lord,
> to whom, with you and the Holy Spirit,
> be honor and glory throughout all ages. Amen.

The hymn, "Now Thank We All Our God" was written during the Thirty Years War and may be used as an example today of how the spirit of thanksgiving can persist even when opposing armies are killing each other off for what they each maintain is Christ's sake.

Proper Twenty-four Sunday Between October 16 and 22 Inclusive

Old Testament Texts

Jeremiah 31:27-34 sketches out a vision of a new covenant. Psalm 119:97-104 offers the boasts of a priest who would keep to the Torah.

The Lesson: *Jeremiah 31:27-34*

What Is New About the New Covenant?

Setting. Jeremiah 31:27-34 has had a long and prominate history in Christian interpretation, starting with the writer of Hebrews, who presents a christological midrash on this text in chapters 8 and 10. According to this author Jesus is new in Jeremiah 31:27-34. Jesus is the new covenant, and this assertion has implications for divine forgiveness and Christian worship. The christological interpretation of Jeremiah is a powerful insight into the text, especially when preaching Hebrews 8 and 10. A problem arises, however, when we too quickly leap to Hebrews to interpret Jeremiah 31:27-34, because both the social context and the theological horizon of this latter text are very different. In view of this, we must bracket momentarily our tendency to interpret the new covenant in Jeremiah 31:27-34 as a prediction of Jesus. With Jesus on hold, we can ask the question, What is new about covenant in Jeremiah? An answer to this question will provide insight into why the author of Hebrews chose to quote the entire text of Jeremiah 31:27-34 when trying to provide commentary on the mission of Jesus.

Structure. Jeremiah 31:27-34 contains two eschatological discourses. The phrase, "the days are surely coming" (v. 27) and "in those days" (v. 29) provide an eschatological setting for a divine word concerning individual retribution in vv. 27-30. The old proverb that the action of parents (eating sour grapes) determines the fate of children (their teeth are on edge) will cease to have proverbial truth. Verses 31-34 sketches out a vision of what will replace the old proverb, once its truth has ceased to influence the divine and human interaction. The repetition of the phrase, "the days are surely coming" in v. 31 provides an *eschatological setting* for the discourse on the new covenant in vv. 31-34. What follows, therefore, is a utopian vision that includes both the Northern and the Southern kingdoms. This is the only place in the Old Testament where the word *new* is used to describe covenant. Verse 32 provides initial *contrast* between the old and new covenants by describing what the new covenant will not be. It is not the covenant of the Exodus which is characterized by two things: disobedience of Israel and God's role as master (Hebrew, *ba`al*—compare the translation "master" with "husband" in the NRSV). Verse 33 switches from the past to provide the *content* of the new covenant. It will be characterized by the internalization of the law into the very character of Israel, with the result that the Lord will be God and Israel the people of God. Finally, v. 34 sketches out the *results* of the new covenant. All will know God and God will forgive.

Significance. The newness of covenant in Jeremiah 31:31-34 does not consist in any of the specific elements listed. The internalization of Torah or law within the hearts of Israel is not actually new—since the law was always meant to be internalized (see Deuteronomy 30:6)—nor is God's ability to forgive a new divine attribute, since this quality was already firmly in place at the time of the Exodus (see Exodus 32). Rather the newness of the covenant consists in the surprising reversals that are referred to in these few verses.

The first reversal is the unexpected ceasation of the statis quo in vv. 27-30. The sins of the parents will not determine the lives of their children. This surprising reversal raises the question of what will replace it. The answer is given in Jeremiah 31:31-34. Scholars debate when Jeremiah 31:31-34 was written. Some attribute the text to the prophet Jeremiah, himself, during the closing days of the monarchy, while others locate it in the late exile or early postexilic period, in which case the writer may be part of later deuteronomistic tradition that is now idealizing the prophet. In either case the vision of an unexpected new covenant creates tensions with the traditional understanding of covenant in the book of Deuteronomy. The language looks to be deuteronomistic (emphasis on exodus, Torah, the heart, covenant, etc.), but it does not conform to the covenant theology of Deuteronomy. At the center of the tension is the belief in deuteronomistic tradition that covenant is conditional upon obedience. This means that God is obligated to Israel only in so far as they adhere to the covenantal stipulations. Jeremiah 11 reflects this deuteronomistic understanding of covenant. Jeremiah 11 asserts that because Israel has broken covenant, God does not want to hear any prayers or petitions for help. The covenant has been broken, and God is now free of all obligations, with the result that Israel will lose the land and go into exile. With such an understanding of covenant, eschatology is impossible once the contract is broken, which means that Jeremiah 31:31-34 should not be in the book. But there it is.

The literary context of Jeremiah 31:31-34 accentuates its inappropriateness with regard to the orthodox understanding of covenant in deuteronomistic tradition, because it has been placed squarely in the setting of the fall of the Southern kingdom, which is the fulfillment of Jeremiah 11 and thus the end of covenant. There are two ways to read the passage, once the paradoxical setting has been noted. One way is to read it solely as a statement about a utopian future, which is disconnected from anything in the past. The newness of the covenant in this case is not a transformation of tradition, but the beginning of new tradition. This understanding of the passage is frequently used in Christian interpretation to talk about Jesus, the new beginning. Another way to read the passage is to bring it into conversation with the orthodox understanding of covenant in deuteronomistic tradition. When read in this way the emphasis on newness is not an attempt to escape the past/present by constructing a utopian future, but the aim is to evaluate critically past orthodoxy because of its power to predetermine what are the limits of God obligations and acts of salvation (see the commentary for last week). When viewed in this way, the passage urges that God can make a new covenant, even though it is not in the theological blueprint of Israel. God can perform surprising reversals.

The readings listed above are essential for interpreting Jeremiah 31:31-34, but there is a logical order for them. The initial focus for interpreting the new covenant within the context of the book of Jeremiah must be the critique of orthodoxy implied in the text, for it is in this reading that the surprising reversals are felt. If anything was clear at the time of the exile, with the destruction of the Temple and loss of land, it was that the covenant was no longer in effect. This conclusion was rooted in deep piety: God has *rightfully* abandoned sinful Israel. Such situations of perceived clarity are the most dangerous for orthodoxy, for they make God too predictable. The new covenant in Jeremiah 31:31-34 undercuts this predictability, and, consequently, it opens up a new and unexpected future with God. The writer of Hebrews saw this characteristic of the text and thus chose it as an avenue to talk about God's unpredictable action in Jesus. The danger for contemporary readers is that what was an unpredictable reversal for the writer of Hebrews has become a well-established orthodoxy. One way to test yourself on whether you have succumbed to the danger of orthodoxy is to check your own reading of Jeremiah 31:31-34. Do you see any surprising reversals here, or is it only a future-oriented text that confirms your already established belief in Jesus? The central aim in preaching Jeremiah 31:31-34 is, first, to evaluate critically the orthodoxy of your congregation and, second, to sketch out new and surprising ways in which God's salvation may be active.

The Response: *Psalm 119:97-104*

How Right Belief Is Derived from Torah

Setting. Psalm 119 is an enormous acrostic poem with every eight lines initiated by one consecutive letter of the Hebrew alphabet, probably as a tool that enable the student to memorize then internalize the ideas. The entire Psalm is a mediation on Torah, most likely (as was Jeremiah) from the priestly class during the Exile. The eight verses chosen here are each initiated by the letter *m (mem)* in the Hebrew alphabet.

Structure. There is not much discernable structure in the subunit, but the psalmist, through a series of escalating boasts, claims that his wisdom is exceptional. The commandments of Torah, when kept diligently, make the psalmist:

1. wiser than enemies
2. more perceptive than his teachers
3. more discerning than the elders (at the gate)

Significance. Several motifs allow Psalm 119:97-104 to function as a response to the new covenant in Jeremiah 31:27-34. The psalmist underscores how the Torah has been internalized personally through meditation, and how it has made her wise, how it has influenced her into action. It emphasizes that an individual who is faithful to the commandments of Torah is likely to exceed the understanding (and holiness) of enemies, teachers, and elders, which is another consequence of implying that children of the new covenant are no longer liable for the errors of their ancestors.

New Testament Texts

The epistle calls Timothy (and us as we listen in) to loyalty to the Christian tradition and to steadfastness in preaching and teaching the good news. The lesson from Luke focuses on a parable Jesus told and subsequently interpreted concerning the importance and dependability of regular, earnest prayer.

The Epistle: *II Timothy 3:14–4:5*

A Call to Faithfulness

Setting. The paragraphing of the NRSV accurately indicates that the verses of this epistle reading are, first, part of a larger appeal made in 3:10-17 and, second, the entire admonition made in 4:1-5. The pastor urges Timothy to loyalty and steadfastness. In the context of this particular epistle we should understand that these directions and appeals are related to the rise of heresy and the rejection of "sound doctrine" by false teachers and their followers.

Structure. The punctuation of critical editions of the Greek New Testament, which is followed by the punctuation of the NRSV, recognizes that there are five sentences in this reading: 3:14-15, 16-17; 4:1-2, 3-4, 5. The thought of these lines essentially evolves as one moves through the reading. First, we find an admonition to remain faithful to what was learned from childhood (3:14-15). Second, the pastor declares the godly value of Scripture (vv. 16-17). Third, Timothy is told to preach and teach with persistence (4:1-2). Fourth, the pastor warns of the danger of rebellious people and false teachers, both groups of whom abandon the truth (vv. 3-4). And, fifth, there is a final charge to faithful ministry (v. 5). The ideas or themes of these statements may be employed in preaching, although the order of the statements can be easily rearranged.

Significance. As the pastor tells Timothy, when that which is of genuine significance is learned, it remains permanently valid and useful. Yet, we can see from the remarks of the pastor that Timothy had made that which he had been taught his own. Firm belief comes as one takes to heart and claims for one's self the lessons of tradition taught by others. In its origin Timothy knew the validity of the facts of his faith from the lives of those from whom he learned. Concretely the pastor may mean to indicate Timothy's grandmother Lois and his mother Eunice (see 1:5), and perhaps even Paul (1:6); but for us the reading may recognize that one of the best "proofs" of faith is a faithful life.

Moreover, as Timothy lived into that which he had learned, his growth in faith came through his being steeped in Scripture. Through a thorough engagement with Scripture Timothy was formed for saving faith in Christ Jesus. We should notice that faith is focused on Christ Jesus, not on Scripture; and salvation is related to faith, not merely to the content of Scripture, which is a vital tool in the life of faith, but it is neither the object of faith nor the subject of salvation. Salvation is found in a trusting relationship to Christ Jesus, and Scripture is a vehicle for mediating much of the basic information of Christian belief. The Pastor's high regard for Scripture is evident in the statement that "all scripture is inspired by God." Commentators frequently point out that "inspired by God" more literally means "God-breathed," and while that is correct, the rest of this striking line makes clear that the pastor's concern is more with the vital function of Scripture than with its nature. As the pastor notes, Scripture is "useful"—useful for teaching, rebuking, correcting, and training in righteousness. Scripture is a sure, authoritative guide in the development of a dynamic life of faith. Indeed, faith formed through Scripture study results in God's people being equipped to do God's will.

The Pastor continues by admonishing Timothy to be diligent and patient in both preaching and teaching, no matter the circumstances encountered. The work of ministry is defined in terms of convincing, rebuking, and encouraging. While the Pastor portrays such activities as Timothy's own ministry, these efforts characterize the faithful living of all Christians. As we live in relation to others, our calling is to provide instruction, positive and negative, concerning God's will and to enliven the faith of others through our own words and deeds. Yet, in the pastor's warning about rambling faithlessness, we see the sad fact that our own faithfulness does not guarantee that we will encounter no problems in life. Nevertheless, despite all difficulties, we are called with Timothy to sensible, steadfast faithfulness—which means doing ministry, that is, to living out God's will.

The Gospel: *Luke 18:1-8*

Never Doubt God's Trustfulness

Setting. The final major section of the account of Jesus' journey to Jerusalem runs from 17:11–19:27. The twin foci of this portion of Luke are discipleship and eschatological expectation. Indeed, disciples are to live in this world being formed and drawn forward by their faith and hope in God's future. The opening verse of our lesson recognizes the vital link between Christian devotion and future hope. The parable of the widow and the judge is peculiar to Luke's Gospel. The point of the parable is clear, although Luke includes further words of Jesus that give particular thrusts to the meaning of the story.

Structure. In v. 1 Luke explains Jesus' motives for telling the parable to his disciples. Then, in vv. 2-5, the basic parable is told. After the telling of the parable, vv. 6-7a and 7b-8 develop two levels of meaning from the simple parable. Thus, we find: introduction, parable, interpretation one, and interpretation two. Luke's introductory remarks and the two rounds of comments from Jesus give us angles from which to view the parable. The preacher's particular situation may make one or more of these angles more pertinent for proclamation.

Significance. The introductory line to the lesson, v. 1, is remarkable. According to Luke, not only does hope in the future invigorate faithful living in the present, indeed, faithful daily living keeps future hope alive. Christian living is a two-way street: The already of the present hopes toward the not-yet of the future, and the not-yet of the future calls forth the hope of the already of the present. Christian faith is profoundly related to the future, but it is thoroughly rooted in the present.

Moreover, Luke informs the reader of his Gospel that prayer is an essential element of Christian life. Prayer is communion with God. As we relate to God, we find our certitude for life in the all-too-uncertain world in which we live. In this world it is easy to lose heart, but through a steady interaction with God we are able to overcome or resist the discouraging fare of daily life. Would-be psychological critics call Christianity "wishful thinking," but wishful thinking is not necessarily unreal. A religion that holds a crucified suffering Messiah at its center is a long way from fantasy and permanent denial.

The parable itself paints a sober picture. The judge is introduced as a man without theological or sociological prejudice. In the contemporary United States of America, that this judge does not fear God may prove to be a credit, that he does not have a social agenda may make him less acceptable. Yet, in Jesus' day and age—a time devoid of the benefits of the separation of church and state—a lack of fear for God was a mark of sheer foolishness. This judge is not neutral, he is godless; he is not necessarily impious, but he is contemptible. Nevertheless, he holds high office and wields great power, so the judge is a formidable figure. In turn, the judge fears no person. At one level this means the judge does not have any strings attached to him. No person calls his number; no one controls his judgments. Yet, the other side of this coin is that the judge is genuinely independent, genuinely self-reliant—in fact, genuinely self-centered and genuinely unconcerned with the normal structures of society around him. The judge does not care about God's commitment to justice, kindness, humility, and love. The judge does not care about human equality. In the crucial terms of his own first-century world, the judge did not care about human honor and shame.

The widow in Jesus' parable appeared before this detached man. Initially the widow's calls for justice were met by indifference. If you don't care about God and if you don't care about people, "Why bother yourself?" But Jesus says that the widow (who perhaps feared God and respected persons) was persistent. The relentless pursuit of justice by the widow paid off, for the judge decided it was better to offer a verdict than to be pestered to death. The very words of the judge illustrate his arrogance, "Though I have no fear of God and no respect for anyone . . . I will grant her justice . . . "; and, not to his credit, these words show that the judge knew right from wrong. Nevertheless, the judge is not the point of this story—though he offers many lessons as asides! Rather, Jesus' parable forms an argument from lesser to greater. If such a reprehensible judge can ultimately do right, what about God? Jesus' teaching is that God can be trusted to heed the valid petitions of those who turn to him in need.

The two comments from Jesus that follow give wider meaning to the parable than the simple sense of the text. First, the declaration in vv. 6-7a recognizes God's faithfulness as it calls forth ceaseless prayer for authentic concerns. Legitimate prayers will be answered according to the teaching of Jesus. Second, God cannot be restricted to the present. God is the God of the present, and God is the God of the future. Humanity lives now in a time already affected by God's work in Jesus Christ, but humanity looks forward to a future moment of time when God will fully realize God's own commitment to justice. After nearly two thousand years, that time seems distant, but Jesus assures us that God's day is coming. For now, our prayers should not pass.

Proper 24: The Celebration

If we are to take seriously the commentary on the lesson from Jeremiah and begin to evaluate critically those reigning orthodoxies that may be blinding us to God's present activity, one way to go is to question the privatistic and individualistic approach to Bible reading and prayer that permeates our culture. In this regard it will be helpful to read Stanley Hauerwas's *Unleashing the Scripture: Freeing the Bible from Captivity to America* (Nashville: Abingdon, 1993). He asserts that contemporary interpreters of Scripture, whether fundamentalist or higher critic, all operate on the premise that the Bible is a book available to individuals who have the right of individual, private interpretation. He maintains that "it is only in the Church that Scripture lives and becomes vivified: [quoting Georges Florosky] 'only within the Church is it revealed as a whole and not broken up into separate texts, commandments, and aphorisms' " (p. 24).

Both lessons from the New Testament (though not the Old Testament readings) today are in one way or another addressed to the community, not to individuals, but our inclination is to read and interpret them privatistically. The admonitions to Timothy are to a pastor in relation to his public ministry in the Church. Does not a doctrine of private interpretation represent the *ne plus ultra* of accumulating teachers to suit their own desires, for who knows what I want to hear better than I? A sermon today may well concentrate on II Timothy 3:16-17 to explore what "all scripture is inspired by God" means in the context of the Church. If that option is chosen, today may be a better choice for the celebration of Bible Sunday rather the one that usually has it competing with Christ the King Sunday. If Bibles are given to children in the church school (a custom that Stanley Hauerwas naturally questions!), it might be done on this day after the preaching of a sermon that has dealt with what it means to read the Bible as a member of the Church.

The Gospel lesson also needs to be interpreted communally, rather than as advice to individuals about spiritually keeping on keeping on. Jesus' words are directed to the disciples (see previously, Luke 17:22), and they need to be heard as advice to the Church about its life of prayer. Liturgy, we remember, means the work of the people, so we are called upon to examine what it means to pray in an ecclesial context. How do we avoid the orgy of self-centeredness that characterizes much public prayer time, and how do we learn to take responsibility for the whole work of prayer of the people of God? What does it mean to rediscover prayer as the Church's expression of faith in the ultimate goodness of God rather than a wish list for people who feel entitled to have their "needs" met? (It is instructive to look at the hymns under the heading of "Prayer" in any hymnal and note how few, if any, refer to prayer as a communal experience.)

A rigorous examination of such questions in light of the "dangers of orthodoxy" interpretation of the first lesson may lead to a liberating renegotiation of the covenant we thought we had with God!

Proper Twenty-five Sunday Between October 23 and 29 Inclusive

Old Testament Texts

Joel 2:23-32 describes how God's actions on the Day of the Lord can change direction or goal in light of Israel's response to prophetic judgment and even result in a new outpouring of divine spirit. Psalm 65 is a hymn.

The Lesson: *Joel 2:23-32*

An Oracle of Salvation

Setting. The reference to the Day of the Lord in Joel 2:1 provides important background for interpreting the Old Testament lesson. The Day of the Lord is not a twenty-four hour period of time. In fact, it is not a definite period of time at all. A better way of thinking about the Day of the Lord is to associate it with a definite divine event in time. The definite event is an action by God that determines the character of the world. The Exodus is such an event or, in the New Testament, the incarnation of Jesus. Such actions are God's Day, and because the events reshape our world there is always a present quality to them.

The Day of the Lord was Israel's way of describing how God breaks into our world in special ways to bring about a new salvation. Scholars debate the particular setting in which the Day of the Lord was first used. It may have been in the context of holy war when Israel saw that real security was not rooted in their military strength but in God. In this context the Day of the Lord was a confession that only the wrath of God could really defeat Israel's enemies. Thus military victory was interpreted as the Day of the Lord, and its celebration required worship, because God's defeat of threatening nations embodied the essence of what salvation meant. Over time the Day of the Lord became one of the central events in Israel's worship, where it was symbolized as bright light. Israel lived for the Day of the Lord. A close analogy in Christian tradition would be an Easter sunrise service, where the light from the rising sun also symbolizes salvation.

Many prophetic oracles presuppose this powerful tradition of salvation. These oracles, however, often use salvation to confront the people of God with their own sin. The Day of the Lord, therefore, is frequently used as a reversal—as a dark and gloomy day of judgment for the people of God rather than the nations. Amos 5:18 provides an early example of this reversal. Here the prophet presents a judgment oracle by stating: "Alas for you who desire the day of the LORD! Why do you want the day of the LORD? It is darkness, and light." Joel 2:1-17 is a prophetic oracle similar to Amos, where the prophet uses a strong tradition of salvation to declare judgment on the people of God for not living out God's salvation. Simply put, the judgment is that God has declared holy war on his own people. But Israel can influence the direction of God's holy war by how they respond to the threat. Because of this fact, Joel 2:23-32 presents a reversal within a reversal, in which God changes direction in order to save rather than destroy Israel in light of their cultic acts of repentance.

Structure. Joel 2:23-32 must be read in the larger context of vv. 18-32, which, in turn, must be interpreted in an even larger context of Israel's cultic acts of repentance in v. 17. The prophetic threat of the Day of the Lord in 2:1-11 led to the proper response of repentance in v. 17, which now elicits a change of direction in God's action toward Israel. Instead of destroying, God becomes jealous for Israel (v. 18). Verse 18 provides an introductory statement about a changed state of affairs in God. The introduction is followed by three divine statements of assurance in vv. 19-20, 21-24, 25-27, which result in a transformation of people (vv. 28-29) and the cosmic order itself (vv. 30-32). The context of reversal is important for preaching Joel 2:23-32, and there is no clue of this if the text is limited to vv. 23-32. Consequently, the preacher may wish either to expand the boundaries of the text or to provide the necessary background concerning the larger context of judgment and repentance in vv. 1-17.

Significance. Verses 19-20 provide the immediate background for the lectionary reading. These verses contain the initial divine response to Israel's plea for forgiveness and for rescue from the judgment of the Day of the Lord. Note how v. 19 reads, "In response to his people the LORD said." The response is in two parts: God will replenish the earth, and thus reverse the drought and locust plagues described in chapter 1, and God will reverse the mythological judgment of the Day itself, which is symbolized by the imagery of the foe from the north.

Two oracles about the earth follow in vv. 21-24 and 25-27. Both represent reversals from images of judgment in chapter 1. Verses 21-24 (of which the lectionary has chosen the final two verses) describe how the drought of 1:16-20 will be reversed. The reason for the reversal is stated in v. 23. It is literally "food or early rain for righteousness" (Hebrew, *hammmoreh lisdakah,* which the NRSV translates less clearly, "early rain for your vindication"). Verses 25-27 describes how the locust plague of 1:4 will be reversed. This unit ends with the statement in v. 27 that Israel will know God. Knowledge of God throws the text into one more reversal in vv. 28-32. This time the reversal is from a picture of the Day of the Lord as judgment to a reaffirmation of its salvific content. Verses 28-29 describe how the outpouring of God's spirit will provide new life for Israel, while vv. 30-32 sketch out the cosmological implications of this new salvation. Joel 2 illustrates how a divine change from salvation to judgment need not be the final word, but can be turned back into salvation through the proper response of the people of God.

The Response: *Psalm 65*

A Hymn

Setting. There is some debate about the form and original unity of Psalm 65. Some scholars argue that the psalm is unified and that it was meant to function as a thanksgiving song of the harvest feast in ancient Israel. Others have suggested that that the psalm originally consisted of two separate hymns, a more communal thanksgiving in vv. 1-8 and a more individual hymn in vv. 9-13.

Structure. Psalm 65 will be interparted as a unified psalm consisting of three sections (vv. 1-4, 5-8, 9-13). Verses 1-4 introduce praise of God on Zion. Verses 5-8 celebrate the power of God as creator from a more universal perspective. Finally, vv. 9-13 narrow the focus down from praise of God's cosmic power to praise of God's ability to deliver rain and to provide bounty.

Significance. The language of Zion at the opening of Psalm 65 provides a direct contact to the closing imagery of Joel 2:23-32 where salvation was also associated with Zion. This point of contact underscores how worship is the setting in which God's salvation is both discerned and celebrated. Psalm 65 clearly anchors the worshiping community in the sanctuary as the place where God's salvation is to be discerned (vv. 1-4). Once the setting of worship has been established, the subject matter of praise ranges from God's cosmological power as creator of the world (vv. 6-8) to God's more immediate power to sustain the created order (vv. 9-13).

New Testament Texts

The readings from II Timothy come to a conclusion as we work with verses from the closing section of the letter. Paul is in peril. He sees no signs of hope in this world, but he remains confident because of his trust in the Lord, who is the foundation of his true hope. In turn, the lesson from Luke 18 is the pointed and profound parable of the Pharisee and the publican. The parable examines the motives for prayer, the nature of prayer, and the results of prayer. We learn that all praying is not equally valid activity.

The Epistle: *II Timothy 4:6-8, 16-18*

Trusting Fully in the Lord

Setting. As noted in relation to the setting of the epistle reading for last week, II Timothy 4:1-5 is a bold admonition to Timothy by the pastor. That "charge" is stated in weighty theological terms, and it is, in fact, the final explicit theological portion of this epistle.

95

Beyond 4:1-5 the theological dimensions of II Timothy are implicit, couched in the more overtly personal statements at the letter's end. The six verses of our reading come from this ending personal section, but with eyes and ears attuned we can see and hear the crucial theological assumptions inherent in these remarks.

Structure. Verses 6-8 state Paul's situation, look back over the course of his ministry, and declare his hope in the face of a seemingly hopeless situation. Our reading vaults over vv. 9-15. Perhaps the framers of the lectionary wanted simply to pass over the references to ancient persons and places that would be obscure to most church members today. (Who is Demas? Where is Dalmatia? How do you pronounce Tychicus? What did Alexander do?) Nevertheless, the omission is unfortunate, for these lines depict in detail Paul's sad situation. Verses 9-15 recognize the failure or weakness of Paul's human support system, and by doing so these omitted lines heighten the statement of Paul's hope: Although humans are in no position to stand by Paul, he is not helpless, for his real hope is in the Lord. Verses 16-18 again recall Paul's past experience, and now even more boldly they state his absolute confidence in his Lord.

Significance. Reading the verses of this lesson by looking for the implicit theological assumptions of the pastor is crucial unless one wants to preach by giving a talk about Paul's purported personal predicament nearly two thousand years ago. In a nutshell, Paul is about to be put to death (v. 6). Paul is facing that fact (vv. 6-7). Moreover, friends and colleagues have abandoned him or they are at a great distance from him (vv. 9-15, 16). Nevertheless, Paul's fate ultimately rests with the Lord, so that whatever the opposition may do to Paul, his real destiny is in the hands of the Lord (vv. 8, 17-18).

Our relationship to the Lord gives us a basis for genuinely free living. Prison, persecution, even execution are merely the worst this world can do to us. Yet, we live in relation to a Lord who is active in this world and whose person and work transcend the boundaries of this life. Because our Lord is larger than life as we currently know it, our relationship to him gives us a source of security that effectively lifts us above the perils of this world. Faith in the Lord produces hope that frees us from the paralyzing fears that can thwart life itself. If we look merely to ourselves, or even to our friends, the basis of our security is limited. We will necessarily be reduced to cautious patterns of life. We will necessarily be reserved in our engagement with and opposition to the forces of evil. To live in any other fashion would be imprudent.

Yet, we do not merely look to this world in charting the course of our lives. We look to the Lord, and in him we find the foundation of freedom. As the pastor knew, because we form our lives in the context of our relationship to the Lord, we can run the risks of faithful service in the certitude that the Lord has promised to preserve us from the forces of evil. Our citizenship is not restricted to the territories of this earth; we are citizens of the Lord's heavenly kingdom. Now, despite life's real difficulties and hazards, we may live boldly and bravely as the Lord's people.

The Gospel: *Luke 18:9-14*

To Whom and How Shall We Pray

Setting. Readers may consult the discussion of setting for last week's Gospel lesson for information concerning the larger literary setting of this week's lesson. More specifically, Luke informs the readers of the setting in the ministry of Jesus from which the parable of the Pharisee and the tax collector came. As Luke tells us, Jesus told "this parable to some who trusted in themselves that they were righteous and regarded others with contempt" (v. 9). Clearly the parable has polemical and didactic value. Since the character in this parable who is "self-righteous" is a Pharisee, Luke may intend to indicate that Jesus told this parable against Pharisees with whom he was in debate—clearly not all the Pharisees as is evident from Luke 13:31. But, since some first-century Pharisees did not have a corner on the market of self-righteousness, we may freely draw analogies to instances of self-righteousness in the life of the church today as we preach from this parable. In thinking of parallels to contemporary experience, the preacher will do well not simply to think of the self-righteousness of the religious "right" or the religious "left," for there are abundant illustrations at both ends of the religious spectrum as well as in between.

Structure. After Luke designates the setting in which Jesus told this parable (v. 9), the parable begins by locating the two characters in the Temple at prayer (v. 10). Initially, Jesus tells how and what the Pharisee prayed (vv. 11-12); then, he tells of the manner and the content of the tax collector's praying (v. 13). Verse 14 completes our lesson, moving beyond the parable to recall Jesus' own pronouncements concerning the meaning of the parable, first, in an overt statement (v. 14a) and, second, in a pithy epigram (v. 14b) that has parallels in Matthew 23:12 and Luke 14:11.

Significance. Few texts are more self-evident than the lines of this lesson. Nevertheless, several details are remarkable and merit attention. First, in his report concerning the setting of this parable (v. 9), Luke indicates that the outcome of persons trusting in themselves (rather than in God) was their having disdain for other people. Self-righteousness yields contempt, not compassion; self-righteousness directs one toward one's self, not toward others. Valid ministry and mission do not come from self-righteousness.

Second, as a good critical commentary will indicate, in Jesus' day the Pharisee would have been regarded as a model of piety. Pharisaic devotion to God's law was thought to be exemplary. Yet, as Jesus' story recognizes, all piety is not equal. Piety can be perverse, although that some piety is rotten does not mean that all piety is vain. Today, piety has gotten a bad name, and it is time to rekindle and reclaim valid devotion. On the other hand, in Jesus' day a tax collector was practically assumed to be a model of sinfulness. Tax collectors were in cahoots with the much hated Roman overlords. They took up the resented Roman taxes, often over-charging, pocketing both the fees they earned and the excess they essentially extorted. Yet, as Jesus' parable informs us, the recognition of sin directs a sinner toward God. Naming sin brings us without pretense before God for redemption and reconciliation. Today we tend to explain our sins away so that we can bring ourselves without sinfulness before God, but our tendency to psychologize, sociologize, and accept sin precludes our experiencing God's grace. Who needs God when we are so efficient at rationalizing our sin away?

Third, Jesus' description of the Pharisee's praying is striking. The NRSV smoothes out the awkwardness of the Greek text and seems to miss the point of Jesus' statement. The RSV was closer to the grammar of the original Greek, "The Pharisee stood and prayed thus with himself"; and the NASB is even better, "The Pharisee stood and was praying thus to himself." In fact, the Pharisee was so content with himself—that is, he so thoroughly trusted himself—that he had become his own God, "not like other people." The prayer of the Pharisee in this parable didn't even make it to the ceiling of the Temple, primarily because his praying wasn't aimed in that direction.

Fourth, the tax collector displayed a genuinely contrite heart. He recognized his own sin and he recognized God's merciful nature. Indeed, we should see that the tax collector's capacity to confess his sinfulness was the result of his recognition of God's graciousness. God's mercy inspires our own repentance and brings us into a right relationship with God. As we know God, we come to know ourselves, and in honest humility we find ourselves "justified." Jesus says that the tax collector "went home . . . justified." He did not achieve justification, nor did he justify himself; he was justified by God, the only one who justifies humanity.

Proper 25: The Celebration

As we begin to draw near to the end of the Christian year the Old Testament and epistle lessons will tend to focus respectively on the Day of the Lord and the Parousia. These will lead to the two final Gospel readings, one from Luke's apocalypse in Luke 21 (where we began our readings on the First Sunday of Advent) and the last on Christ the King Sunday where, from Luke's Passion narrative, we see Christ reigning from the throne of the cross. An underlying theme for these Sundays of late October and November as nature seems to be dying (in the northern hemisphere, at any rate) is the inevitability of death and the restoration of all things in Christ. That, of course, is the very message of the Easter cycle and helps demonstrate how all liturgy is finally a commentary on the meaning of Christ's death and resurrection.

The lesson from Joel is part of that quoted by Peter in his Pentecost sermon (Acts 2:17-21) and was seen by Luke as a description of the Pentecost event. For Luke the Day of the Lord dawned at Pentecost, and since then the church, as does Paul in the epistle reading, waits for its full and final appearance.

The Gospel reading can effectively be done as a mini-drama that requires only a narrator and two others to portray the Pharisee and the tax collector. The narrator should read (or tell the story) from the pulpit or lectern or near the front of the congregation; the Pharisee's lines should be delivered near the altar or other place of prominence in the church, and the tax collector's from the back pew. After the original recital, there could be replays using parallel figures and lines from contemporary life—for example, an environmental activist carrying an appropriate placard ("I recycle all my garbage and never drive my car when I can walk") and an ax-carrying logger, or a right-to-life protester ("I stand in the picket lines three days a week and have been jailed for obstructing clinics more times than I remember") and a scapel-carrying physician. Try to balance the political elements, so that the self-righteousness of both the left and the right are recognizable. The point is to bring home to the congregation the radical character of the parable as it was first heard from the lips of Jesus. The preacher needs to remember that the point of the parable has not to do with the right or wrong of tax collecting, logging, or performing abortions, but what it means to be justified by God. Notice that Jesus doesn't cater to his hearers' prejudices or seek to win them over by saying that because he had been justified the tax collector found another job. How is the radical impact of the parable a kind of "Day of the Lord" experience to the hearer?

The preacher might wish to explore the difference between the Pharisee's boastful catalog of attainments in the parable and Paul's own list of his accomplishments. How does Paul's self-knowledge (humility) save him from the Pharisee's fate?

Proper Twenty-six Sunday Between October 30 and November 5 Inclusive

Old Testament Texts

Habakkuk 1:1-4; 2:1-4 frame a dialogue between the prophet and God about divine justice during chaotic times. Psalm 119:137-44 are a meditation on the reliability of God's righteousness.

The Lesson: *Habakkuk 1:1-4; 2:1-4*

Standing on the Watchtower

Setting. Little is known about the prophet Habakkuk. The opening lament of the prophet in Habakkuk 1:2-4 concerning injustice and the divine answer in 1:5-11 concerning the rise of the Chaldeans (i.e., Babylonians) would suggest that the prophet lived and prophesied during the closing years of the southern kingdom of Judah, since the Babylonians only enter Judean politics after they defeat the Assyrian empire in 612 B.C.E. The political turmoil of this period provides important background for interpreting the book of Habakkuk. Certainly the Judeans were no lovers of Assyrians, since the Assyrians dominated Judaen political life for nearly two hundred years. Yet the Babylonians will also prove to be a ruthless power, and it is, in fact, they who will bring to an end the Judaen nation in 587 B.C.E. driving Israel into exile. The oracles of Habakkuk in 1:1–2:4 raise questions of divine justice and providence with regard to Israel's fortunes in the waining years of the Judean kingdom.

Structure. The lectionary has included the beginning (1:1-4) and the end (2:1-4) of a dialogue between the prophet and God, which requires the larger context of 1:1–2:4 for proper interpretation.

101

After the opening superscription in 1:1 where the prophet is identified, 1:2–2:4 separates into four parts. Chapter 1:2-4 is a complaint
by the prophet concerning injustice by Israelites. In this complaint
the prophet asks God why justice must go forth crooked and how
long this situation will continue. God answers the prophet in 1:5-11
by stating that the Chaldeans (i.e. Babylonians) will be one form of
divine response to injustice within the Israelite community. Rather
than providing an answer to the prophet's lament, God's raising up
of the Babylonians provides the occassion for an additional lament
by the prophet in 1:13–2:1. Here the prophet questions whether it
is just for God to punish Israel with the seemingly more evil Babylonians. The section ends in 2:2-4 with God's reponse to Habakkuk's
second complaint. This answer is in the form of a vision. The entire
section of Habakkuk 1:1–2:4 can be outlined in the following
manner:

I.   Superscription (1:1)
II. First Complaint and Divine Response
     A. Complaint Concerning Injustice Within Israel (1:2-4)
     B. Divine Response: The Coming of the Babylonians
        (1:3-11)
III. Second Complaint and Divine Response
     A. Complaint Concerning the Divine use of the Babylonians
        to Punish Israel (1:12–2:1)
     B. Divine Response: The Need for a Vision of the End
        (2:2-4)

Significance. Habakkuk 1:1–2:4 is about clairvoyance. The
superscription in 1:1 prepares the way for this concern by noting
how the book is about Habakuk's "vision," where the technical
Hebrew term for clairvoyance is used (Hebrew, *hzh;* NRSV "saw").
What does Habakkuk see around him at the present time? And what
is the content of his vision in light of what it is that he has presently
seen?

What does Habakkuk see? Motifs of sight appear throughout
1:1–2:4. Of particular note are the combination of two Hebrew
words, "to see" (*r'h*) and "to look at" (*nbt*) in each of the first three

sections. These verbs underscore how Habakkuk sees tensions between the evolution of human history and the character of God. This tension raises a question for the prophet of why God doesn't act more decisively against human action that conflicts with the divine character. The first occurrence of the Hebrew word pair is in the lament of the prophet in v. 3, where Habakkuk states: "Why do you make me see (Hebrew, *r'h*) wrong doing? and you (presumably God) look at (Hebrew, *nbt*) trouble?" That Habakkuk sees: (1) he is aware of evil around him as a result of being forced to see it by God ("Why do you make me see wrong doing?") and (2) he knows that God is also looking at the evil ("And you look at trouble?"). The combination of these two points of insight (that evil has distorted reality itself and that God is aware of the distortion) gives rise to the opening question, "O LORD, how long shall I cry for help, and you will not listen?" The opening section makes it clear that the book of Habakkuk is not about human doubt in God. Rather it is a problem of knowledge that accompanies faith—namely, the insight by the faithful that God tolerates evil. This insight prompts the prophet's second question: Why do you look at trouble?

The divine response to the prophet in 1:5-11 begins by picking up the two verbs of sight in v. 5. God commands the prophet: "See (Hebrew, *r'h*) the nations and look at (Hebrew, *nbt*) [them]!" Here Habakkuk learns that God intends to use the Babylonians to address the problem of perverted justice within Israel. But this new insight only prompts more questions from the prophet in 1:12–2:1. Note particularly how the problem of what God sees returns in the prophet's discourse in v. 13: "Your eyes are too pure to behold (Hebrew, *r'h*) evil, and you cannot look on (Hebrew, *nbt*) wrongdoing; why do you look on (Hebrew, *nbt*) the treacherous, and are silent when the wicked swallow those more righteous than they?" In other words, as far as the prophet is concerned, fighting evil (injustice within the Israelite community) with evil (the Babylonians) does not measure up to the purity of vision that should eminate from God's eyes. Given the tension between the distortion of human events and divine purity, silence cannot be God's final response to this situation. And, in view of this, the prophet stations himself on the watchtower in

2:1 and states: "I will keep watch to see (Hebrew, $r'h$) what he would say to me."

What is the content of Habakkuk's vision? The verbs of perception give way in 2:2-4 to the language of vision, when the technical word for prophetic clairvoyance from 1:1 returns in 2:2 with the divine command: "Write the vision (Hebrew, hzh)!" The vision is a snapshot of the end of time. Verse 3b underscores how the quality of this end-time vision is secure. The prophet learns that even if the picture tarries in coming into focus within human history, it is worth waiting for, since "it will surely come, it will not delay."

Verse 4 provides the content of the vision, which is itself about insight. The NRSV translation reads: "Look at the proud! Their spirit is not right in them, but the righteous live by their faith." This is a very difficult text to interpret primarily because of the word that the NRSV has translated "proud." The Hebrew, *'uppelah,* occurs only in Habakkuk 2:4 in its present form, and only one other place in the Old Testament—in the story of the spies in Numbers 14:44, where it is best translated, "to act heedlessly." A summary of the events surrounding Numbers 14 may provide help for interpreting Habakkuk. The spy story is about Israel's inablity to see the goodness of the land. In this narrative twelve spies are sent into Canaan, and, upon their return, only two, Joshua and Caleb, give a good report of the land, stating that God would surely help them in claiming the land as their inheritance. The ten other spies and all of the Israelites could not see the goodness of the land because of their fear of the Canaanites, prompting them to refuse to enter Canaan. Yahweh enters the story at this point and, in view of Israel's prior refusal, also refuses to lead them any further, which prompts Israel to change their minds about entering Canaan. Moses discourages Israel from proceeding toward Canaan because God was no longer in their midst to protect them or to fight for them, but Israel charges ahead any way. In the story of the spies the verb "to act heedlessly" is used to describe Israel's decision to march ahead toward Canaan even though God was no longer in their midst. The action conveys a certain headstrong blindness, which results in their destuction by the Amalekites. Perhaps the vision of Habakkuk is also about such action and the inevitable results that it brings. The "proud" in the NRSV translation would then also be understood as those who act with a headstrong blindness that inevitably results in their destruction. With this as background, the point of the vision is made through a contrast. Persons who do not pay attention to the tensions between God and human history that the prophet has seen—that is, who act heedlessly—are themselves distorted ("their spirit is not right in them"). Over against these persons, the righteous (those like the prophet Habakkuk who see the tension between the character of God and human history) must live by faith—that is, by their insight into the character of God. The reliability of the end-time vision underscores that the end of human history will confirm the choice of the righteous even when it creates tension in the present time.

The Response: *Psalm 119:137-44*

A Praise of Divine Justice

Setting. Psalm 119 is an elaborate acrostic psalm of which the section vv. 137-44 is initiated by the Hebrew letter, *sade,* on every line of poetry. Many scholars categorize Psalm 119 as a wisdom psalm.

Structure. Psalm 119:137-44 does not separate clearly into smaller sections.

Significance. The section is dominated by praise of God as the source of Torah. The primary attribute of God that arises from the praise of the psalmist is divine righteousness, which might be better understood or translated into our vernacular as divine *justice.* God's law puts things right, even in the face of trouble or suffering.

New Testament Texts

The epistle reading is the first of a series of three readings from II Thessalonians. The lines utter the most basic and essential kinds of theological convictions. The lesson from Luke is the beloved story of Jesus and Zacchaeus, a story lesson about the operation of grace.

The Epistle: *II Thessalonians 1:1-4, 11-12*

The Hope of God's Sustaining Grace

Setting. I and II Thessalonians are remarkably similar, but quite different, documents. (Scholarly debates over the Pauline authorship of II Thessalonians are vigorous and result in an almost even split in the conclusions interpreters draw about Paul's writing this letter.) In II Thessalonians there seems to be a crisis in the church related to eschatological teachings. According to the epistle someone has said that the Day of the Lord has already come (2:1-2), and this teaching has been accepted by some of the Thessalonians so that others are now unsettled and alarmed. In I Thessalonians Paul taught that the Day of the Lord "will come," so the Thessalonians were to live in hope, encouraging one another. Now, however, someone has said that the day of the Lord "has already come"; and so, some of the Thessalonians have ceased working, for if the Day of the Lord has come Christians living on earth are liberated from all bodily cares. Why work if the glory of the day of the Lord has already arrived? Rather, some say, live at ease.

Structure. The lectionary suggests an unusual cluster of verses for our epistle reading this Sunday. Verses 1-2 form the salutation of the letter, naming the senders (Paul, Silvanus, and Timothy) and the recipients (the church of the Thessalonians), and issuing an opening greeting (v. 2). Then, vv. 3-4 are the first two verses of the thanksgiving of the letter (1:3-12); whereas, vv. 11-12 are the final two verses of the same. In part the lectionary committee seems to have followed the paragraphing of the NRSV which starts a new paragraph with v. 5, but as Greek texts recognize and punctuate, vv. 5-10 are part of a single "run-on" sentence in Greek that begins with v. 3 and ends with v. 10. The suggested omission avoids the seemingly harsh tone of vv. 5-10, which articulate a reward and retribution scheme. Yet, we should notice that the severity of the lines is an expression of the connection between the real afflictions the Thessalonians are said to have endured and God's concern and ultimate authority over their situation. Moreover, by omitting vv. 5-10 the reading loses the crucial eschatological cast that informs the meaning of vv. 1-4, 11-12. Preachers may decide to read all of vv. 1-12.

Significance. In form, the salutation (v. 1-2) is a standard greeting for a Hellenistic letter. It is one of the briefest and least elaborate of the greetings in Pauline letters. Several items, however, merit attention: First, the letter is the product, somehow, of joint-authorship. Second, the Thessalonians are called "church," a Greek word that both described Greco-Roman political assemblies and was used in the Septuagint to designate the assembled Israelites in their desert wanderings and in Temple worship. *Church* here refers to a local congregation, not the church universal. Third, the Thessalonian church is located "in God the Father and the Lord Jesus Christ," a phrase that qualifies the Thessalonians' existence theologically as well as geographically. Fourth, the titles given to God and Jesus Christ are striking. Naming God as "Father" conjures thoughts of "creation theology" and evokes the ideas of permanence, intimacy, and dependability. Moreover, God as "Father" is a concept from Jesus' ministry. In turn, naming Jesus as "Lord" recognizes his majesty, power, and rule. While the Greek word for "Lord" could mean "Sir," it was the manner of referring to Caesars, and it was the Greek word used in the Septuagint to translate the Hebrew name for God, *YHWH.* Fifth, "grace and peace" refer to God's work in Jesus Christ and the results of that work. Here, God's effort and achievements salute the Thessalonians rather than a mere "Greetings."

Taken together all these items remind us that Christianity is not an individulistic existence. We live the life of faith both in relation to other believers and in relation to our God and Lord. We are called as church to be located in this world, but we have our true identity and live in the presence and the power of God and Christ. The simple statement of being "in God the Father and the Lord Jesus Christ" is loaded with the creation and redemption motifs of salvation.

The verses of the thanksgiving-prayer hold a wealth of material. In vv. 3-4 Paul and his colleagues give a report of their thanks to God for the Thessalonians. Moreover, we find that they boast of the faith and steadfastness of the Thessalonians among other congregations. The faithful suffering of the Thessalonians serves as inspiration for other Christians in other places. Thus, suffering is not glorified or rationalized, but even though it is unjust suffering, it does not remain pointless. Verses 5-10 verbalize a reward and retribution scheme. In context these lines seek to encourage the Thessalonians. Beyond the tit-for-tat level of the statement there is an utter confidence in the authority of God. The present does not determine the future; rather, God's promised future already pronounces righteous judgment on the present itself. Faith in God brings hope to bleak circumstances. In turn, vv. 11-12 assure the Thessalonians of the apostles' prayers for them. God's sustaining grace will strengthen the Thessalonians so that their faithfulness will glorify the name of the Lord Jesus Christ.

The Gospel: *Luke 19:1-10*

Zacchaeus, Today's the Day

Setting. Information concerning the literary setting of this week's lesson appears in the discussion of the setting of the Gospel lesson for Proper twenty-four. As Jesus journeyed to Jerusalem he passed through Jericho, and a crowd gathered around him. In the midst of that popular assembly Jesus acted in an amazing way—that is, amazing to the crowd. He singled out Zacchaeus, a chief tax collector, and invited himself to Zacchaeus's house for the day. Jesus' deliberate activity surprised and shocked the crowd, the members of which expressed their incredulity and displeasure with Jesus' actions. Nevertheless, the ensuing words spoken by Zacchaeus and Jesus are still more surprising and revealing of the will and the work of God.

Structure. Luke 19:1-10 is an extremely well-told story. The basic storyline of the account of the meeting of Jesus and Zacchaeus suggests a number of themes for preaching. Consider the following: Seeking to see Jesus; diligence in the quest despite difficulties; being called by Jesus; Jesus' surprising pattern of relations; human transformation in the presence of Jesus; generosity as a liberated response to grace; the breadth of salvation, its scandal and glory; and the purpose of Jesus' ministry.

Significance. Children sing about Zacchaeus. Most folks know his story, having heard or even told it repeatedly. Despite our familiarity with and fondness of the story of Zacchaeus, the account is often misunderstood because of contemporary society's tendency quickly and easily to psychologize the characters in biblical narratives. Both Bible studies and sermons tend to explain away the gospel of this account. The following remarks are aimed at fostering an appreciation of the story for itself.

Zacchaeus turned out among the members of the crowd to see Jesus. This is not merely a matter of shallow curiosity. Luke tells us plainly that Zacchaeus wanted to see "who Jesus was." Zacchaeus's question concerning Jesus was about his identity. *Who* was this that had preached, taught, healed, exorcised, and raised the dead?

The report of Zacchaeus's diligence often encourages misreadings of the text. Luke tells us that Zacchaeus was a chief tax collector, that he was rich, that he was short, and that he climbed a tree so he could see Jesus. Sermons sometimes suggest that Zacchaeus had an inferiority complex because of his stature, so he overcompensated by amassing wealth. Jesus' love freed Zacchaeus from his complex. Thus, Jesus was the first psychologist. There is, however, nothing in this story to suggest that Zacchaeus had a complex. In fact, a first-century Palestinian Jew would not have known what a complex was.

Instead of psychologizing, let us see what Luke does tell us. Zacchaeus was rich. He got rich by working as a big-time tax supervisor for the Romans. The people didn't like Zacchaeus, not because he was rich (ordinarily most ancients would have assumed wealth signified divine blessing), but because he worked for the Romans. Zacchaeus went to work for the Romans and became terrifically rich. If this means anything, it means that Zacchaeus had few social or religious scruples, and he was obviously greedy. With that in mind, let us see that Jesus Christ loved Zacchaeus anyway. That is the gospel. Even self-centered greed isn't beyond the boundaries of God's love made present in Jesus Christ. .

Zacchaeus wondered who Jesus was, and then he found out that Jesus was the one who reached out to those whom others assumed to be off God's list. Jesus said, "I *must* stay at your house today." What compelled him to do so? In v. 10 Jesus answers this question, "The Son of Man came to seek out and to save the lost." As the agent of God's judgment ("Son of Man") Jesus Christ mediated the presence of God's saving grace. God's grace reclaims those who have come to be outside the parameters of polite religion, doing for them what they cannot do for themselves. God's grace always does for us humans what we cannot do for ourselves—it saves us.

As Jesus reached out to Zacchaeus and Zacchaeus came into the context of saving grace, we find that Zacchaeus was transformed. Luke says Zacchaeus was joyful. (The words rendered in the NRSV as "was happy to welcome him" literally say, "he received him rejoicing.") This man who heaped up a fortune was suddenly moved by the gracious presence of Jesus to generosity beyond belief. Zacchaeus did not merely tithe, he gave away half of all that he had. Moreover, he promised to set straight anything he had done wrong.

Jesus' unconventional behavior is a display of God's grace that grasps our lives and transforms us into lovely reflections of the godly grace we experience as salvation. Zacchaeus posed the question, Who is this Jesus? Now we know that Jesus Christ is the active bearer of God's saving, transforming grace.

Proper 26: The Celebration

The commentator's observation above about the opening of the Second Letter to the Thessalonians that "God's effort and achievements salute the Thessalonians rather than a mere 'Greetings' " prompts some reflections on how we begin our worship services. It is increasingly popular in some churches to use the term *Greeting* for what was once the "Call to Worship." Unfortunately the term has been equated with its use in the secular society and frequently ends up as little more than the pastor and people saying "Hello" to one another. The use of "Good morning" to introduce the liturgy, while it has all the appearance of comfortable amiability, does nothing to assert the unique character of this time and place as one where the People of God gather for the special purpose of participating in the rehearsal and remembrance of God's saving action. The church gathers not for the sake of reinforcing its own society (although that is a byproduct of the event) but to encounter the living God in the proclamation of the Word and sharing of the sacred meal. It is "God's efforts and achievements" that should greet us and begin to focus the reason for our gathering. This can best be done by the use of scripture sentences, delivered solo or responsively, that are chosen with care to help frame the occasion in relation to the lessons that will be read later or the particular time in the Christian year. *The Presbyterian Book of Common Worship* (Louisville: WJKP, 1993) contains sets of opening sentences for each Sunday in the year for all three years of the lectionary. It also has separate opening prayers for the Sundays of all three years.

An excuse sometimes given for not using the lectionary is that there is not enough time in the service for all those readings. The reason for that may be that too much time is spent on other things such as, for instance, the entrance portion of the service. A choral introit and a responsive call to worship are redundant. If the service begins with a processional hymn it is, in effect, the call to worship, and all that is needed after that is a brief scriptural salutation between pastor and people before the opening prayer or an invitation to confession before the prayer of confession. The entrance rite should not give the impression of an exercise in mood setting!

The issue of the suffering of God's people and what God intends to do about it is at the heart of both the Old Testament and the epistle lessons. Important and helpful reading in theodicy for a sermon on these texts could include Stephen T. Davis, ed., *Encountering Evil: Live Options in Theodicy;* Wendy Farley, *Tragic Vision and Divine Compassion: A Contemporary Theodicy;* Douglas John Hall, *God and Human Suffering: An Exercise in the Theology of the Cross;* John Hick, *Evil and the God of Love;* and S. Paul Schilling, *God and Human Anguish.*

The concluding verse of the Gospel lesson is quoted in Charles Wesley's poem written shortly after his conversion, "Where Shall My Wondering Soul Begin."

Outcasts of men, to you I call,
harlots and publicans and thieves;
he spreads his arms to embrace you all,
sinners alone his grace receive.
No need of him the righteous have;
he came the lost to seek and save.

The first line could be altered to "The world's outcasts . . . " and the stanza could be sung as a solo response to the reading of the Gospel lesson. Possible tunes are Carey's (Surrey), Fillmore, Melita, and St. Catherine.

111

All Saints Day November 1 or First Sunday in November

Old Testament Texts

Daniel 7:1-3, 15-18 is the account of Daniel's vision of the four beasts who come up from the sea. Psalm 149 is a two-sided hymn of praise in which God's ability to destroy and to save is acknowledged.

The Lesson: *Daniel 7:1-3, 15-18*

Glimpsing the Destiny of the World

Setting. The use of Daniel on All Saints in Year C is the only occurrence of this book in the entire three-year cycle of the New Common Lectionary (Daniel occurs twice as an alternate reading in Year B for Propers Twenty-eight and Twenty-nine). The book of Daniel is characterized as an apocalypse. Such books tend to be pseudepigraphic literature (the author is not named) that idealize great individuals. The genre flourished in the Hellenistic age and later. Given the characteristics of the genre Daniel is most likely not the author of the book but an individual who is being idealized to represent how a wise Jew might function in the Hellenistic age. The genre of apocalypsis often presupposes a time of crisis for its intended audience, in which the purpose is to place a historical conflict in a larger perspective that includes supernatural forces. Hence a time of persecution on earth may be framed within a larger world view in which a parallel conflict in heaven is described. The larger perspective often provides the stage for the writer to encourage his or her audience by showing them that the present crisis will not last forever and that, even though it will most likely not be solved by human forces, one day the supernatural forces of good will overcome the present evil. Because of the tendency of apolyptic literature to present the "big picture" of reality, it often incorporates suprahistorical imagery with highly mythological content in order to convey how heavenly forces are also involved in the conflict of earthy communities. The vision of Daniel 7 certainly fits in well with these tendencies. Daniel has a vision about earthly kingdoms (or beasts) that have arisen from the sea and terrorize the community of faith. Behind this vision is some form of earthly crisis to the community of faith, be it Antiochus Epiphany or some other foreign ruler or regime in the second-temple period. These kingdoms, however, provide windows into a heavenly scene, where divine forces pronounce judgment on the earthly beasts.

Structure. The book of Daniel stands out because it is written in two languages. Daniel 1:1–2:4a and 8-12 are written in Hebrew and chapters 2:4b–7:28 are written in Aramaic. Whether there is a significance to the distinct languages in interpreting the book is difficult to say, since the overall structure of Daniel does not follow exactly the separation of languages. Instead, the book of Daniel breaks into two parts, with chapters 1-6 recounting tales about the character Daniel, and chapters 7-12 presenting a series of visions by him. Furthermore, scholars of Daniel suggest that the division of the book into chapters 1–6 and 7–12 provides a clue to a series of smaller correspondences in the literature, with the result that chapters 2 and 7 deal with four kingdoms, chapters 3 and 6 recount miraculous deliveries, chapters 4 and 5 are critical of Babylonians kings. Even such a brief sketch of the outline of the book brings to light the central role of chapter 7. It is the first chapter of visions and appears to occupy a central role in the overall design of the book.

Daniel 7 can be separated into the following parts:

I. A vision in which four beasts provide an allegory of history (vv. 1-8)
II. A vision of judgment on the four beasts in heaven (vv. 9-12)
III. The transfer of the heavenly judgment to earth through "one like a human being" (vv. 13-14)
IV. Interpretation of the vision to Daniel (vv. 15-22)

V. Interpretation of the fourth beast (vv. 23-27)
VI. Conclusion (v. 28)

Significance. The outline indicates how the lectionary text includes aspects of the opening vision (vv. 1-3) and interpretation (vv. 15-18). The preacher or liturgist may wish to expand the reading to incorporate more of the transhistorical imagery in the text, especially as a springboard for reflecting on All Saints. The power of the text is in its mythological imagery and how this imagery is a more reliable interpreter of historical reality than our experience at any one time. This insight surely goes to the heart of All Saints.

Whatever the exact historical crisis may have been that prompted the writers of Daniel to produce the book, the imagery in Daniel 7 and its message are fairly clear. The message is that, for the people of God, historical crises must be interpreted on a transhistorical stage. As a result, for the community of faith conflict is not simply an historical problem but also a cosmological problem. And it is on the cosmological plain that the people of God must ultimately evaluate the course of their lives and history as a whole. For the writers of Daniel, the destructive earthly kingdoms are part of a larger problem of mythological chaos, which goes back to the origin of creation, itself, where the chaotic sea was in conflict with God's desire to bring order into the world. These destructive earthly powers, therefore, must be interpreted in the larger context of the chaotic sea— God's ancient opponent in the struggle for creation. The vision describes how the heavenly battle against chaos will be won and that the results of this victory will influence earthly communities. This is made clear when the judgment in heaven (vv. 9-12) is brought to earth through the "one like a human being" (vv. 13-14). The inevitable result of linking the heavenly and earthly victories is that the saints (those persecuted in the present time throughout history) will inevitably one day have dominion in a world where the divine order for creation will be common place. All Saints is a celebration of this future fact. This celebration pushes us beyond our immediate struggles and joys and puts our collective life in a more realistic framework that includes God's larger struggle against evil.

The Response: *Psalm 149*

A Call to Praise

Setting. Psalm 149 is a hymn of praise that evolves into a call for the worshiping community to participate in a Holy War against the nations. The language of Holy War takes center stage in vv. 7-9a where the faithful are called to wreak vengeance on nations, to bind kings, and to execute judgment. ·

Structure. Psalm 149 separates into two parts that can be outlined in the following manner.

   I.   A Call to Sing a New Song (vv. 1-4)
       A. Call to Praise (vv. 1-3)
       B. Reason for Praise (v. 4)
  II. A Call to Praise God and Participate in Holy War (vv. 5-9*a*)
       A. Call to Praise (vv. 5-6)
       B. Call to Holy War (vv. 7-9*a*)
 III. Conclusion (v. 9*b*)

Significance. Psalm 149 has strong undercurrents of Holy War. It is a call to arms. The people of God are clearly contrasted against the nations and encouraged to defeat and destroy them. When Psalm 149 is read as a response to Daniel 7 the potential nationalistic overtones of the hymn give way to the cosmological conflict that is sketched out in the vision of Daniel. Within this framework what stands out is that the celebrated victory is rooted in the activity of God. It is praiseworthy because of the certainty that God will achieve his ends. In this sense Psalm 149 celebrates the future fact of divine victory in the present context of the worshiping community.

New Testament Texts

The text from Ephesians combines declarative lines concerning the spiritual blessings believers experience in Christ and a grand expression of thanksgiving that recognizes and celebrates God's saving power in Jesus Christ. The epistle reading is elegant, inspiring, and challenging for proclamation. In turn, the lesson from the Gospel is a portion of Jesus' Sermon on the Plain, offering parallel materials to portions of Matthew's Gospel. First, one encounters Luke's version of the Beatitudes. Then, the lesson combines Luke's briefer version (than Matthew's) of Jesus' blessings with a set of woes and a series of explicit instructions about the goodness, graciousness, and generosity that are to characterize the life to which Jesus called his disciples (notice the focus at the beginning of the teachings in 6:20).

The Epistle: *Ephesians 1:11-23*

Thanking God for the Riches We Have in Christ

Setting. Normally Pauline letters open with a greeting, as Ephesians does in 1:1-2, and then follows a prayerful thanksgiving prior to the beginning of the body of the letter. Ephesians, however, has a blessing of God for the blessings Christians have received (similar to a Jewish *berakah)* in 1:3-14; and then, 1:15-23 is the usual thanksgiving prayer report. The lection offers a running start at vv. 11-14, which provide the reason for the thanks in prayer.

Structure. There are three broad, related movements in the lesson: First, in vv. 11-14, Ephesians offers two reasons for giving thanks:

1. We have been destined and appointed to praise.
2. We have been sealed by a promise of the Holy Spirit.

Second, in vv. 15-19, hearing of the believers' faith in the Lord Jesus and of their love of the saints, Ephesians gives thanks for the believers and asks that God may give the believers a spirit of wisdom and revelation resulting in the knowledge of God for their illumination into hope (part of God's call), for an awareness of their inheritance among the saints, and for an appreciation of God's great saving power.

Third, Ephesians shifts the focus in vv. 20-23 to comment on God's mighty working in Jesus Christ. Thus, the meditation takes a christological turn, both remembering and declaring

1. God's resurrection of Christ,
2. God's exaltation of Christ over
3. all powers and places,
4. all names in all times, and
5. God's making Christ the head of his body, the church, which now shares the benefits of his glory.

Significance. The opening verses, vv. 11-14, come from a psalm-like pronouncement (1:3-14) that offers a doxology to God. The mood of glorifying God may well characterize the beginning of a sermon on this text. Before considering the ideas of "choosing" and "destining" (Presbyterians should take heart from this passage!), it is well to consider the phrase *in Christ* for Ephesians says it is in Christ that believers are "chosen" and "destined for adoption." Small seas of ink have been spent spelling out the significance of *in Christ*. Some interpreters take the phrase as a synonym for *in church*, while others relate *in Christ* to a form of Christian mysticism. The plain sense of the phrase in Ephesians is spatial. To express this sense of *in Christ* we may paraphrase, "in the context of the new creation established by the powerful grace of God at work in the life, death, and resurrection of Jesus Christ."

The statements that God chose and destined us for adoption "in Christ" make clear that it is by God's work and into God's family that we are brought by God's grace. These lines convey a remark-able message about God, about God's work in Christ; and only sec-ondarily do they provide information about us. The point of this pas-sage is that God works graciously through Christ for our benefit. The author is not interested in defining who is chosen and why, or who is not chosen and why not. The lines are theological, not anthropological, because the good news celebrated here is about God. The gospel has meaning for us, but it is not about us. There-fore, we must be careful with this potent text!

The lines from the thanksgiving of the letter (1:15-18) unpack the meaning of God's blessings for us as believers and members of the church. The prayer asks that God give the believers the gift of inti-mate comprehension of God. Such understanding is not knowledge that comes through human ingenuity or effort—such as knowledge which comes from studying a math textbook. Rather, Ephesians asks for the gift of God's self-disclosure, which would come as an ever-deepening relationship between God and the believers. This kind of knowledge is charismatic and mysterious and comes as God works in our lives, not as we grasp after unseen things. In relation to God, the life of believers is characterized by the joy of hope and an awareness of the richness of God's grace. Believers have a new attitude, but it is not the result of positive thinking; it comes purely as a gift from God, and it activates a new way of living. Verse 19 makes this clear by speaking of "the immeasurable greatness of his power for us" and of "the working of his great power."

With this mention of God's magnificent power, the thanksgiving takes a christological turn to illustrate the clearest testimony to God's power—namely, the resurrection of Christ. As is normal in New Testament thought, Ephesians refers to the resurrection as something that God did. Though Christology articulates and illustrates the truths of God, God never takes the backseat to Jesus Christ. This manner of thinking is the pattern of early Christian reflection, and from time to time we have to remind ourselves that the glory of divine radiance emanates from God, lest we lose sight by blocking God out with a "Son umbrella." As we meditate on Christ, we ponder the greatness of God.

The passage continues by recalling the range of Christian conviction in relation to Christ, speaking of his exaltation, his power of all other powers, and his relationship to the church, which participates in his majesty. As the first mention of God's power in v. 19 stated that it was/is "for us," so now in v. 22 we read that God "has put all things under [Christ's] feet and has made him the head over all things for the church." In this christological mediation, which ultimately celebrates the powerful work of God, there is a deep conviction that what God has been about in Christ has profound significance for the church. This idea often causes discomfort for Christian theologians living and working in comfortable settings, for the passage seems "triumphalistic" or "self-aggrandizing." But we have always to recall that these lines we most likely composed when Christians did not have any worldly power and, in fact, were facing opposition and persecution. Far from celebrating current power and status, these lines are a critical statement of faith about God's grace and generosity that would sustain believers in difficult circumstances. We should avoid using these lines to excuse our tendency toward living in luxury.

The Gospel: *Luke 6:20-31*

"Blessed are . . ."

Setting. The presence of the statements beginning with "Blessed are . . ." explains, in part, the selection of these verses for All Saints Day in year C. As Professor McCabe astutely observes, "The Gospel lesson provides an agenda for growth in sanctity." Our lesson comes immediately after one of the several special moments of prayer by Jesus in Luke's account (5:12). The result of this particular experience through prayer was that Jesus chose and named twelve special disciples, called apostles (meaning "ones sent out"). This action recognizes the time and nature of Jesus' ministry in relation to God's eschataological work for the salvation of humanity, for the twelve seem to symbolize "eschatological Israel," the very hope of God's promise of salvation.

This portion of Luke's "Sermon on the Plain" (Luke 6:17-49) is a collection of Jesus' teachings comparable to elements of Matthew's more extensive "Sermon on the Mount" (Matthew 5–7). The verses of this week's lesson may be compared with Matthew's Gospel in the following way:

Luke	*Matthew*
vv. 20-23	5:3, 6, 11-12
vv. 24-26	no parallel
vv. 27-30	5:39-42
v. 31	7:12

Structure. The lesson falls into four sections, vv. 20-23, 24-26, 27-30. As the crowds came to Jesus, the first portion of the lesson recalls four "beatitudes" and a prophetic pronouncement made by Jesus. Second, coupled with these teachings, the next section records four "woes" stated in counterbalance or antithesis to the foregoing blessings. Then, from comparison of Luke and Matthew we see that the final verses of our lesson fall into third and fourth sections. Verses 27-30 articulate the important themes of nonretaliation and generosity; v. 31 offers Luke's version of the well-known Golden Rule. Thus, our complex lesson brings us blessings, woes, and challenging directions for life—all in an eschatological context. For preaching one needs to establish at the outset of the sermon a sense of expectation and urgency typical of eschatology and, then, in that context reflect upon the contents of the lines of the lesson.

Significance. Jesus' teaching here in Luke is not "dressed up" and it is very straightforward. Jesus talks of real poverty, of real hunger, of actual weeping, and of being hated and excluded. In relation to these terrible experiences Jesus speaks of the will and the work of God to overturn these situations. Poverty, hunger, sorrow, and oppression are contrary to God's purposes, and Jesus' promise is that these condemnable realities will not prevail. It is crucial to notice at least in relation to the fourth item—being hated and excluded—if not in relation to all these conditions, that the horrible experience comes because of the relation of persons to "the Son of Man." Fidelity to God may come at a heavy price, but God will have final say about the condition of those who are loyal!

On the heels of the blessings come the words of woe. As the blessings were pointedly related to reality, so are the woes. Jesus issues warnings to the rich, the full, those who laugh, and those of whom others speak well. From Jesus' own involvement with Zacchaeus, at banquet-tables, and in celebrations we should be wary, however, of concluding that he speaks here as the original mean-spirited Puritan. Again we must take these liens in relation our disposition or fidelity to God. This understanding is warranted by the final reference to "the false prophets." Thus, Jesus says that if we live in this world forming our loyalties with an eye toward enjoying this world's benefits, we should be prepared to undergo God's judgments for our lack of faithfulness to God's own purposes.

The warnings here follow the promises of blessings, and we should see that in the first place the lesson issues a call to us to be faithful to a faithful God. Only in the second place, but there, the lesson warns us against false priorities. Thus, for preaching we should give emphasis to the positive dimensions of the text, although some recognition of the reality of God's eschatological judgment as well as God's eschatological salvation is necessary for a thorough engagement with this lesson.

Above all, we cannot reduce these verses to morality, especially to private morality. This is clear from the text. All the you-language of the lesson is in plural form. Jesus talks of God, calls humans to God's ways, and speaks to the disciples (see v. 17 and v. 20) as an assembly. From these insights, the sense of the lesson is fairly straightforward. The calls to nonretaliation, generosity, and mercy in vv. 27-31 are based on God's own nature and on the assumed reality of the relationship of Christians to God. To be God's children is to relate to others as God relates to us. Jesus' teaching here is essentially positive in thrust.

All Saints: The Celebration

The lessons for today have a pronounced eschatological flavor, and it is to be observed that the same is true for the Sunday lessons from now until Advent where, on the First Sunday of Advent, the return and triumph of Christ is especially celebrated. One could almost call November the "season of All Saints" because the lessons spend so much time dealing with the salvation that will come to the People of God ("the Holy Ones" in today's Old Testament lesson) when evil has been finally overcome.

It is important to emphasize in this celebration that the saints in the biblical sense include all of us who have been baptized, who have been set apart, which is what *holy* means, by the work of Christ in our baptisms. The issue is not whether we are saints; it is what kind of saints we are. The Gospel lesson provides an agenda for growth in sanctity.

The hymn, "Ye Watchers and Ye Holy Ones," is a perfect hymn to begin the All Saints Day service and to use to make the point that all of us saints are involved, in heaven and on earth, in the service and the worship of God. The first stanza is addressed to "all the company of heaven," which includes the angels in all their various ranks: watchers and holy ones (Dan. 4:13,17), seraphs (Isa. 6:2-6), cherubim (Gen. 3:24), thrones, dominions, princedoms, and powers (Col. 1:16), virtues (variant of powers in Col. 1:16), archangels (Jude 9), and angels (Gen. 28:12). The second stanza is addressed to the Virgin Mary who, as the Queen of Heaven, is "higher than the cherubim" and "more glorious than the seraphim," and who is called on to lead the angelic choir. We know that it is Mary who is being addressed because it is she who is the "bearer of the eternal Word," who was called "full of grace" (most gracious) by the angel Gabriel, and who in her earthly life made it her business to "magnify the Lord" (Luke 1:46). This stanza is a direct paraphrase of the "Hymn to the Mother of God" sung at the close of each choir office in the Greek Church. The third stanza then calls on everybody else in heaven to join the choir! The faithful dead, including the patriarchs and prophets, the Twelve and the martyrs are all invoked to participate in praise. Then, at last, the rest of us ("I have called you friends") are invited to unite our voices in the cosmic hymn of praise to the Trinity. This hymn can be found in *The Hymnal 1982* (Episcopal), no. 618; *The Lutheran Book of Worship,* no. 175; *The Presbyterian Hymnal,* no. 451; *The United Methodist Hymnal,* no. 90, and *Worship* (3rd edition), no. 707.

Depending upon the size of the congregation, candles may be placed in the chancel or around the altar, and a candle lighted for each name as the names of those who have died during the past year are read.

The Eucharist is appropriate for today because in that meal we join "with all the company of heaven" in anticipating the heavenly banquet. Baptism is also appropriate today since in that act others are incorporated into the roll of saints.

Proper Twenty-seven Sunday Between November 6 and 12 Inclusive

Old Testament Texts

Haggai 1:15b-2:9 is the second oracle of the prophet Haggai concerning the construction of the Jerusalem Temple after exile. Psalm 145 is a hymn of praise.

The Lesson: *Haggai 1:15b–2:9*

Temple Construction and the Presence of God

Setting. The oracles of Haggai take place for five months during the second year of the reign of Darius I, who was a Persian monarch that ruled from 522–486 B.C.E. The oracles of Haggai, therefore occur in the year 520 B.C.E., which is the early post-exilic period of ancient Israel.

Structure. The book of Haggai is structured around precise dates in the second year of the reign of Darius. The opening section of the book begins in the second year of Darius, the sixth month and the first day (1:1). On this day Haggai calls for the rebuilding of the Temple, which begins on the sixth month and the twenty-fourth day (1:15*a*). The second section begins in the second year of Darius, the seventh month and the twenty-first day (1:15*b*) when the prophet announces future divine blessing on Israel and the future grandeur of the Temple. The third section begins in the second year of Darius, the ninth month and the twenty-fourth day (2:10) when the prophet questions the priests about clean and unclean matters associated with the Temple and concludes by prophesying the future glory of Zerubbabel as the one to continue the Davidic dynasty. The outline illustrates how the lectionary text is limited to the second section of the book.

Significance. The central message in Haggai's preaching is the rebuilding of the Temple. In fact the prophet goes so far as to suggest that drought and poverty would be reversed if the people would only build the Temple (1:1-15*a*). Such an emphasis on the construction of a building to ensure divine presence is difficult for contemporary Christians because it appears to be a mechanical view of religion—if the people would only build a Temple, they would acquire both God and wealth. One is reminded of the phrase from the movie, *Field of Dreams,* where the central character keeps hearing a voice saying, "If you build it [a baseball field in his cornfield], he [the main character's dead father] will come." The book of Haggai might be subtitled, Temple of Dreams, since he appears to be proclaiming that if post-exilic Israel will only build the Temple, God would come. But such a conclusion is premature. If we look more closely at what the Temple symbolized for Israel and also at the historical circumstances of the people in the early post-exilic period, the message of Haggai takes on more complex dimensions.

An understanding of the theological significance of the Temple requires a brief summary of the southern kingdom of Judah's theological tradition of Zion that is rooted in King David. Zion theology was built on two confessions of divine election. The first was God's election of David to be king over Israel with the promise that David's line would rule forever. The second confession was God's election of the Temple in Jerusalem as his permanent home. These two confessions of divine election can be described as being unconditional—that is, their reliability and security rested on God's guarantee and not on human obedience. Psalm 132 summarizes this belief system, when God's election of David (vv. 11-12) and choice of the Temple in Jerusalem (vv. 13-15) are celebrated.

The Babylonian exile of 587 B.C.E. was a direct challenge to the theological foundations of Zion. When Israel sang the lament in Psalm 137:1, 4 ("By the waters of Babylon—there we sat down and there we wept when we remembered Zion . . . How could we sing the LORD's song in a foreign land?) they were not expressing homesickness, but the despair of people in the midst of a religious crisis. The exile called into question Israel's central confession of faith: the Davidic king was deposed by the Babylonians, and even more shocking, the Temple—the house of their God—was destroyed. The fall of the Temple, in particular, left the people with the troubling question: Was Marduk, the God of the Babylonians, the true God, since the Babylonians overpowered Judah and their God? And, even if an exilic Jew did not become a Marduk worshiper, the sticky question remained of how God could possibly dwell in the midst of exilic Israel without the Temple to channel the divine presence. Psalm 137 expresses this problem with the rhetorical question, "How shall we sing of the Lord's song in a foreign land?"

The victory of the Persians over the Babylonians in 538 B.C.E. was interpreted by Haggai and other exilic prophets as a sign of God's renewed action in world events, because it allowed the people of Judah to return to their homeland and provided an answer to the troubling question about the presence (or more accurately the absence) of God. The return of the people to Jerusalem would once again provide a channel for God to dwell in the midst of the people as had been the case before the exile. The return from exile, therefore, was interpreted as the dawn of a new age for Israel, which would be marked by a new level of divine presence and blessing. Such expectations are the background for Haggai's urgent proclamation concerning the building of the Temple. The building of the Temple is urgent for at least two reasons to the prophet.

First, the building of the Temple is urgent because the prophet saw from world events that God was already on the move ushering in a new age. Hence there could be no delay in constructing the Temple as a response to the divine activity. In just a short time, Haggai tells the people, God would shake the nations of the world and the foundations of creation itself. The Temple must be ready for such divine action.

Second, the building of the Temple is urgent because the action of God in world events alone does not guarantee the realization of the divine presence for Judah. The people must also respond to the divine presence and show that they are fit for worship. They must build the Temple and provide a safe channel for themselves to worship God who is already active in their midst. When Haggai's message is viewed within the larger context of Zion theology, the construction of the Temple has less to do with conjuring up God's presence for one's own self-interest, since God is already present and on the move. The construction of the Temple has more to do with whether post-exilic Israel could keep up with God at this point in time. Building the temple was one way in which Israel was able to get on God's train before it left them behind in the station.

The Response: *Psalm 145:1-5, 17-21*

A Song of Praise

Setting. Psalm 145 is yet another example of an acrostic psalm, in which letters of the Hebrew alphabet provide a loose structure for composition. Furthermore the psalm looks to be the song of an individual where it was meant to function within Temple worship.

Structure. The structure of Psalm 145 is difficult to determine. Many scholars break the psalm in half, with vv. 1-9 being followed by vv. 10-20 and v. 21 providing a conclusion. Within this larger structure it is also possible to isolate smaller units. For example vv. 1-2, the call to praise by an individual, would appear to be followed by a reason why God is praiseworthy in v. 3. The pattern of call to praise and reason for praising God may also be present in vv. 4-9 (call for Israel to praise in vv. 4-7 and reason for praise in vv. 8-9) and in vv. 10-13a (call for all creation to praise in vv. 10-12 and reason for praising God in v. 13a). All of the possible divisions noted here suggest that the verses designated by the lectionary need revision, since vv. 1-5 and 17-21 do not reflect natural breaks within the psalm.

Significance. Psalm 145 is a sustained call to praise God, with a focus on the praiseworthiness of God's kingdom. Furthermore the act of praise spreads out as the hymn progresses. It begins with the "I" of the speaker in vv. 1-2 and moves to the people of God in vv. 4-7 before taking on universal dimensions in vv. 10-12. In appropriating this hymn for worship the ever-increasing circles of praise should be taken into account in determining which portions of the psalms will be used.

New Testament Texts

The epistle reading meditates on the work of the Lord among the Thessalonians offering thanks to God, admonishing the Thessalonians to continued faithfulness, and praying for the Lord to bring about what the apostles ask the Thessalonians to do. The lesson from Luke recounts a controversy in the ministry of Jesus concerning the reality of resurrection. Jesus' words teach about the meaning of resurrection for humans, but more, they tell about the person of God.

The Epistle: *II Thessalonians 2:1-5, 13-17*

Facing, Pondering, and Praying About the Life of Christian Faith

Setting. The discussion of the setting of Proper Twenty-six's epistle reading offers information about the "setting in life" to which II Thessalonians is related. More specifically, the reading for this Sunday is ten of the twenty-two verses of the body of the letter (2:1–3:5), which falls into three parts. First, the initial twelve verses (2:1-12) offer an inexact schedule of events leading to the coming of the day of the Lord. Second, 2:13-17 is a thanksgiving that precedes the third and final segment of the letter (3:1-5) which offers an admonition to the readers. Our lesson is two slices of the letter's body.

Structure. II Thessalonians in 2:1-5 presents a vague schedule, containing no exact temporal references, looking toward the day of the Lord. The lines aim to "settle down" the Thessalonians, to assure them of the veracity of teachings that had been presented to them by Paul, Silvanus, and Timothy at an earlier time. Then, in 2:13-17 we find a thanksgiving of sorts. Here the authors explain the reason for their thankfulness—namely, that God chose to save the Thessalonians. In this thanksgiving report there is an exhortation (v. 15) and a benediction (vv. 16-17). Thus, the dynamics of vv. 13-17 are thanksgiving, exhortation, and blessing. In striving to impart a mood of eschatological assurance, preachers may find the logical pattern of these final verses as inspiring as the contents for the construction of a sermon.

Significance. The inexact timetable of 2:1-5 simply seeks to assure the Thessalonians that, no matter what they have heard, the day of the Lord has not yet transpired. First, we read that there will be a "rebellion"; then, "the lawless one," "the one destined for destruction" will appear. These lines are a striking instance of early Christian "anti-Christology"—the notion of a cosmic foe who makes overt the reality of invisible spiritual warfare being already waged between God in Christ and the forces of evil. In thought and language the passage is similar to Revelation 20, and one preparing to preach on this passage will do well to consult critical commentaries and Bible dictionaries, for members of the congregation may have more questions about this reading than can possibly (or, profitably!) be addressed in the sermon. Above all, one should notice that the text is consistent with other New Testament apocalyptic echatological scenes in that it does not hint *when* the events being foretold will occur. The mystery of the future remains a mystery; what is unknown is simply unknown.

As vv. 13-15 inform us, when the apostles thought of the salvific experience of the Thessalonians they had to turn to God and give thanks. The coming of the Thessalonians to faith, their spiritual growth, and their steadfastness in faith were all the results of God's working among them. Observing the Thessalonians compelled the apostles to recognize God's work and to give God thanks for the Thessalonians' salvation. Yet, it is not only to God that the apostles have a word to say. Observing the Thessalonians' faithfulness moves the apostles to admonish the Thessalonians to remain faithful to what they had been taught. We should remember that someone has introduced distorted eschatological teaching into the life of this church, and in large part II Thessalonians is attempting to correct a problematic situation. Thus, this call to hold to the traditions is both a call to affirm the earlier teaching of the apostles and a call away from the new thinking to which the Thessalonians had been exposed. Thus, we see that issues of orthodoxy arose even in the earliest decades of the church's existence.

The blessing pronounced in vv. 16-17 implicitly recognizes the authority of Jesus Christ over the life of the church and the loving devotion and care of God for the church. Christ's authority and God's care are the sources of comfort for the Thessalonians, and because Christ reigns and God loves, the Thessalonians have the assurance that the Lord will give them stable lives that are characterized by good words and deeds.

The call for prayer recognizes the importance of mutual concern on the part of believers. Christians are to pray for one another. As the apostles prayed for the Thessalonians, so now they call for the Thessalonians to pray for them. It is God's care for both the Thessalonians and the apostles that makes their lives and ministries fruitful. Lest the Thessalonians misunderstand that the apostles are asking them to do something unreasonable, the apostles declare their faith in the Lord's own faithfulness. That for which the apostles call for the Thessalonians to pray is, indeed, what the apostles believe.

The Gospel: *Luke 20:27-38*

The Question of the Resurrection

Setting. Luke's account of Jesus' journey to Jerusalem concluded at 19:27. We move into the final major unit of the Gospel in 19:28. Here, in 19:28–21:38, Luke reports the work of Jesus in Jerusalem prior to his Passion. The story of Jesus Passion, death, and burial is told in 22:1–23:56. The Gospel according to Luke comes to its conclusion with Luke's telling of the events of Easter day in 24:1-53. Our lesson clearly comes in the section of stories about Jesus' work in Jerusalem.

Luke's record of Jesus' debate with certain Sadducees over the idea of resurrection runs from 20:27-40. This account is Luke's version of a story also told in Mark 12:18-27 and Matthew 22:23-33. Luke's story is distinct in (1) not including a denunciation of the Sadducees, (2) offering the lines found in vv. 34*b*-35*a*, and (3) including the concluding remarks in vv. 39-40. The lectionary suggests leaving off the final approving statement by some scribes in v. 39 and Luke's own editorial report in v. 40. Deleting these two verses does no harm to the original story, although simply reading these lines to finish Luke's whole story will add but seconds to the time required for presenting the Gospel lesson.

Structure. The story moves in four parts. First, v. 27 introduces both the Sadducees and the topic of resurrection. (The break between vv. 27-28 is slightly different in the Greek text from the versification of the NRSV.) Second, vv. 28-33 lay forth the Sadducees' elaborate question. Third, vv. 34-38 recall Jesus' answer, wherein vv. 34-36 make a straightforward statement of his understanding, which is validated by scriptural argumentation in vv. 37-38. Fourth, vv. 39-40 conclude with a comment from the scribes and Luke's remark to the readers. The flow of the narrative—situation, question, answer, reasoning, conclusion—provides a logic that may inform the structuring of a sermon on this lesson.

Significance. A few facts help in preparing to preach in relation to this lesson. The Sadducees were extremely conservative theologically. They disregarded all biblical writings that were later than the five books of Moses. Thus, they had no textual basis for affirming the resurrection, unlike the Pharisees who both valued later prophetic and wisdom literature and depended on oral tradition as an authoritative basis for theology. Jesus' teachings consistently show him to be closer to the beliefs of the Pharisees than those of the Sadducees. As Jesus arrived in Jerusalem, we find the Sadducees coming out to test his orthodoxy.

The Sadducees did not simply ask a question, they presented Jesus with a "case" about which he was asked to make a decision. This hypothetical case resulted from the Sadducees' imaginative reading of Mosaic laws of levirate ("brother-in-law") marriage in relation to the idea of resurrection. In v. 28 the Sadducees quote Deuteronomy 25:5 in part, offering a freely stated version of the law. The Sadducees' case seeks by means of *reductio ad absurdum* to disprove the reality of resurrection. Today, many people have problems believing in the resurrection, but we should note the difference between contemporary doubters and the Sadducees. The Sadducees had a fixed notion of religious authority that led them to deny resurrection; today's doubters typically attribute their reservations concerning resurrection to some scientific preconception about the nature of life. It is striking that narrowly focused religion and so-called open-minded science can produce the same reaction to certain religious teachings. Neither the Sadducees nor supposedly scientific modern persons seem to recognize that their own systems of belief are filled with unexamined commitments.

Jesus' answer starts by drawing a clear distinction between life in this world and the resurrection life of God's future. Profound transformation of the quality of life occurs in the transformation from life here-and-now and life in the eternal presence of God. The Sadducees' reasoning was flawed because they started with faulty assumptions. Their flawed logic would never grasp the reality of resurrection. Remarkably, for us today the surest assurance we have concerning the reality of the resurrection comes from our faith in Jesus Christ, faith in his teaching and faith in the revelatory reality of his own resurrection.

As Jesus continued to speak, however, his "exegesis" shows that even Moses perceived the great truth that life itself (and the reality of resurrection) is founded in God; life is not merely resident in humanity. Perceiving the truth of God gives us at least the possibility of perceiving the truth of resurrection. God's eternal character, God's eternal love, God's eternal faithfulness are the security of God's own people. Therefore, through faith in Jesus Christ, we "live into God"; and we find the foundation of our hope in the reality of resurrection. God's work in Jesus Christ is the basis of resurrection faith.

Proper 27: The Celebration

Paul's exhortation to "hold fast to the traditions that you were taught by us" in today's epistle lesson presents an occasion to explore the place and meaning of tradition in the church's life. The currently popular differentiation between tradition as the living faith of the dead and traditionalism as the dead faith of the living can help relate the text to the celebration of All Saints Sunday if that occurs today and the preacher elects to use these texts rather than those for All Saints Day.

Superficially it may appear that there is a conflict here between Paul's appeal to tradition and Jesus' condemnation of uncritical fidelity to human traditions (see Matthew 15 and Mark 7). In fact, it is Jesus' criticism of the tradition that has become the new tradition! The Gospel lesson illustrates how Jesus deals with traditionalism by subjecting it to a theological dynamic that is rooted in the eternal character, love, and faithfulness of an eternal God (see commentary above).

The congregation may be accustomed to hearing tradition referred to in a negative way, so it will be important to emphasize that the church cannot do without tradition since it is part of our corporate memory. The Bible itself begins with an oral tradition; how we read and interpret it is a question of tradition. Even being nontraditionalist becomes a tradition! The issue for the church is not the existence of tradition, but how it is used to inform our life in the present.

The rebuilding of the Temple is a case study in applied tradition. See the above commentary.

It may be interesting to note that these reflections on tradition occur at the point when both church and culture are about to begin the celebration of a whole series of holiday traditions. The preacher may be able to use the congregation's attachment to some of their local traditions as a way of seeing themselves in the role of the Sadducees and so help them experience the radical nature of the text rather than hearing it as a dull account of a dated theological debate.

The Temple image in Haggai suggests the use of "Christ Is Made the Sure Foundation" for the opening hymn. The theme of tradition as a living faith expressed in present action can be reinforced by the hymn "Forward Through the Ages." II Thessalonians 2:16-17 may serve as the dismissal that precedes the blessing.

Proper Twenty-eight Sunday Between November 13 and 19 Inclusive

Old Testament Texts

Isaiah 65:17-25 is a vision of God's new creation. Isaiah 12 is a hymn of thanksgiving.

The Lesson: *Isaiah 65:17-25*

Where Is This New Creation?

Setting. Isaiah 65 is part of a larger section of the book of Isaiah (chapters 56–66) that is attributed to a post-exilic prophetic voice, designated Third Isaiah. Isaiah 56–66 share much of the imagery of the seventh-century prophet, First Isaiah or Isaiah of Jerusalem (chapters 1–39) and the exilic prophet, Second Isaiah (chapters 40–55). There is an emphasis on the creative power of God and on the importance of Jerusalem or Zion as the focus of God's creative and saving activity. One of the differences between the three parts of the book of Isaiah concerns Israel's changing historical circumstances. First Isaiah prophesied before the exile when the first Temple was still standing and the salvation symbolized by Zion was considered to be a present reality. Second Isaiah sought to reinterpret Zion tradition in the context of the exile, especially toward the end of the exilic period where the presence of God in world events appeared so clear to the prophet that he began to predict a return to Jerusalem as an imminent event and how such a return would usher in a utopian era.

The voice of Third Isaiah is located back in Jerusalem after the return from exile. Third Isaiah is less optimistic than Second Isaiah. In the post-exilic period, the predictions of the exilic prophet, Second Isaiah, have been realized. Jerusalem and the Temple have been rebuilt. But it has not ushered in the utopian era envisioned by Second Isaiah. In fact, many who would have identified with Second Isaiah have found themselves persecuted in the post-exilic period. Thus the present focus of Second Isaiah concerning an imminent utopian era for post-exilic Israel fades. Where the prophetic voice of Third Isaiah still echoes the perspective of the earlier visions of Second Isaiah is by the way in which the latter prophet projected the utopian age into a future vision of a whole new creation. Isaiah 65:17-25 sketches out what such a new age will be like.

Structure. The larger context of Isaiah 65 is important for interpreting the lectionary passage. Isaiah 63:15–64:12 is a lament by the prophet about the seeming absence of God in the post-exilic period. Injustice is taking place and God appears to do nothing about it. Isaiah 65 is the divine response to the prophets complaint, which separates into three parts. In vv. 1-7 God responds that he was, indeed, ready to be called upon by post-exilic Israel, but the majority of Israelites sought the divine in other ways that prevented God from being present. This section ends with God promising judgment (vv. 6-7). Isaiah 65:8-16 qualify the divine judgment because of the faithfulness of a remnant, who are designated as God's servants (v. 8). This section closes with God sketching out the blessings that await his servants (vv. 13-16). The lectionary text in vv. 17-25 provides the reason why the promised blessings of God are reliable. God's blessing are sure because he is the creator.

Significance. Isaiah 65:17-25 is a divine speech, in which God calls attention to a frenzy of creative activity that is already beginning to take place. Isaiah 65:17 conveys the mood with language that is immediate. The technical verb "to create" (Hebrew, *bara'*) is only used with God as the subject and in v. 17 the participial form of the verb pulls the creative activity into the present time. J. D. W. Watts (*Isaiah 34–66,* Word Biblical Commentary, vol. 25 [Waco: Word Publishing, 1987], p. 349) captures well the immediacy of the text when he translates v. 17: "Indeed, look at me; creating a new heaven and a new land." What follows are large brush strokes of the central characteristics of this new world order, which is brought into view through a series of contrasts. Infants will not die prematurely, but live to be one hundred years old. Houses will not be built by one person only to be taken over by someone else. Instead, those who build will live in their own dwellings. The same is true for land. The one who plants is the one who will harvest, which leads into a broader contrast, namely that all work will be purposeful. And finally humans will be fertile, producing many descendants. The contrasts concerning quality of life give way in v. 24, when the relationship between God and humans is described. Here God states that the intimacy between the divine and humans will be so intense that he will answer before people even make requests. This imagery negates the opening divine complaint in Isaiah 65:1 that God was ready to respond to humans, but no one made a request. Such intimacy between God and humans transforms the cosmos itself, so that the natural order of violence between wolf and lamb or lion and ox also gives way to peace.

This certainly is a powerful vision, but the question remains of how one preaches such a utopian text without sounding socially naive or appearing to be an otherworldly escapist. The fact of the matter is that the world we live in is not like this. The only place where such a utopian vision of a new creation can be proclaimed with integrity is in the context of the worshiping community itself. But even in the context of worship one must be careful where the focus lies, since the community of faith does not embody the cosmological harmony that is pictured in Isaiah 65:17-25. Such a vision is sacramental in character and hence must be rooted in God, who makes worship possible and is at its center. The divine proclamation of a new creation that is already in the process of formation provides an excellent opportunity for the preacher to explore the meaning of the Eucharist as a messianic banquet in God's new creation, especially how God is present in the sacrament before we even ask. Once the present reality of God's new creation is proclaimed in preaching and once the worshiping community participates in this new order through the sacrament, then the present reality of Isaiah's utopian vision can provide a springboard for ethical action outside of the worship setting without requiring that the people of God be naive to the violence that characterizes much of our present world.

The Response: *Isaiah 12*

A Hymn of Thanksgiving

Setting. Isaiah 12 is a hymn of thanksgiving, which has eschatological overtones by the repetition of the phrase, "you will say on that day," in vv. 1 and 4.

Structure. The repetition in vv. 1-4 provides a starting point for structuring the hymn of thanksgiving. The first address in v. 1 introduces a series of thankgivings in the first person ("I will give thanks. . . . I will trust. . . .") The second address in v. 4 leads to more communal praise. Hence the hymn can be read in two parts, but one may also wish to single out v. 3 as a separate unit between two sections consisting of vv. 1-2 and vv. 4-6. Verse 3 takes on prophetic overtones about joy that are realized in a cultic ritual that includes drawing water from a well.

Significance. Isaiah 12 provides an excellent response to the vision of new creation in Isaiah 65 because it claims the reality of that vision with more personal imagery. The "I" statements put the promises of salvation into the voice of the congregation, where the cosmological imagery of a new creation is transformed into the more personal imagery of the Exodus. Note how vv. 1-2 repeat language from Exodus 15 where God's salvation was celebrated by Moses and Miriam.

New Testament Texts

The verses from II Thessalonians issue a blunt call to proper patterns of Christian living. We learn that Christian life is to be active, not idle, for we are called to service, not to being served. The Gospel lesson comes from Luke's version of Jesus' teachings about the future. These verses are quite challenging, for at one level they are related to history as we know and experience it, but at another level the lines are extremely apocalyptic and eschatological.

The Epistle: *II Thessalonians 3:6-13*

The Right Kind of Christian Living

Setting. A full discussion of the situation addressed by II Thessalonians appears in the materials for Proper Twenty-six. The verses for this Sunday's epistle reading come from the parenetic portion (direct, practical advice) that follows the body of the letter. Indeed, the parenesis runs from 3:6-15, so that our reading takes in everything but the last two quite historically specific verses of the parenesis. While vv. 14-15 are pointedly related to the situation addressed by II Thessalonians, the crucial value of these verses is that they show that winning those in error back as brothers and sisters in Christ is more important than merely winning. Although the lectionary does not suggest reading vv. 14-15, the important point they score should inform the interpretation of the preceding verses of parenesis.

Structure. The advice in vv. 6-13 falls into three parts: v. 6, vv. 7-10, and vv. 11-13. First, we find a commandment to the Thessalonians to shun any member who remained idle and, thus, disobedient to the basic Christian tradition. Second, the apostles call for the Thessalonians to imitate the work ethic of the apostles. Third, the apostles address the idle members of the Thessalonian church directly, telling them to get busy with worthwhile activities and not to remain idle and active as mere busybodies. The reading forms a three-part call to appropriate action. A sermon on these verses may find direction by taking seriously the bold tone and the dynamic call.

Significance. The apostles turn to the Thessalonians giving them a command. The language of command has a military tone in Greek, which is enhanced by the reference to the Lordship of Jesus Christ and the words translated "living in idleness." The Greek word rendered as "living" literally means "walking" and the Greek word translated "idleness" literally means "in an irregular, disorderly manner," referring to the conduct of troops. That this disorderly manner of living amounts to idleness is clear from vv. 11-12. The apostles declare the disorder of idleness to be out of keeping with the heart of Christian tradition. By invoking the name of the Lord Jesus Christ the apostles recall the life of Jesus, which itself shows the godly patterns that should characterize the lives of Christians.

Furthermore the apostles call for the Thessalonians to imitate the example of industriousness that the apostles themselves provided for the Thessalonians. Paul especially could call for his converts to imitate him because, as he explained in I Corinthians 11:1, he lived his own life in imitation of Christ. Thus, to follow the concrete example of the apostles was to follow the way of living manifested by Jesus Christ. As Christ labored, giving himself in faithful service to God for others, so the apostles lived and worked, providing an example for their congregations to follow. Here, the apostles articulate a clear, deliberate religious work ethic. These verses are not a call to labor for the achievement of salvation, but they are a frank recognition that Christians are called to live out their lives as faithful testimonies to the Lordship of Jesus Christ. Finally, v. 10 declares a stringent standard, yet at the heart of this stern statement is a conviction that each and every believer is called to do her or his share of the necessary work of the Christian community.

Verses 11-13 turn toward, not on, the idle. The apostles candidly assess the unacceptable behavior of some of the Thessalonians. Such candor is difficult today, but the church needs to recapture something of the reality of telling the truth in love, of correcting one another in love. Again, these verses invoke the authority of the Lordship of Jesus Christ in redirecting the troublemakers who are called back into line under the direction of Christ. Verse 13 issues an injunction, literally, "May you never tire of doing good." This call addresses both the industrious and the idle in Thessalonica. The industrious are to keep on doing what they have been doing; the idle are to get back to it.

The Gospel: *Luke 21:5-19*

Jesus Speaks About the Future

Setting. A discussion of the literary dimensions of the final episode in Luke's Gospel (19:28–24:53) occurs in last week's materials. We find ourselves still in Luke's account of Jesus' work in Jerusalem. After Jesus' controversy with the Sadducees over resurrection (last week's lesson), his teaching denounced the scribes for their exorbitant legal fees and their pretense. Then, Jesus taught his disciples about the quality, rather than the quantity, of pious devotion and generosity. Our lesson follows on the story of the widow's offering and takes a thoroughly futuristic orientation, looking toward both a forthcoming earthly and an eschatological time.

Structure. Several distinct elements make up our lesson. First, vv. 5-6 speak of the destruction of Jerusalem. Second, vv. 7-9 seem to relate initially to that catastrophe, but ultimately prove to be related to the *eschaton*—that is, to the day of God's final judgment of the world. Third, vv. 10-11 continue to speak in dramatic apocalyptic language of the cosmic catastrophic events leading up to the final judgment. Fourth, in vv. 12-19 Jesus talks in relatively plain terms about the real difficulties the disciples are sure to suffer before the end—perhaps before the ends—that is, before both the destruction of Jerusalem and the day of final judgment. Not only are the disciples promised persecution, they are assured that their Lord Jesus Christ will sustain them despite the hardships they will meet.

Significance. It is crucial for valid comprehension to distinguish the elements related to the destruction of Jerusalem from the elements concerned with final eschatological judgment in these verses. Yet, that the earliest Christians saw some relationship between these two times provides insight for thinking about preaching on these verses. Future events, historical and eschatological alike, fall ultimately under the authoritative judgment of God.

Jesus' words about the Temple recognize a sobering truth. Nothing, not even the glorious dimension, of this world has a sure future. Indeed, even the most glorious portions of our humanly constructed world are subject to destruction and destitution. Jesus' teaching underscores this point, and with our own eyes we see the same truth affirmed in abandoned and ruined churches all over the world—sometimes in our own neighborhoods. True spiritual sanctuary is not granted in physical structures, even the most noble cathedrals. The security of transcendent divine authority cannot be boxed, even in houses of worship. The most glorious religious architecture is but a symbol of the glory of God. While our symbols are subject to the destructive forces of this world, we confess that God is not simply vulnerable to the forces of evil. God's struggle with evil moves slowly, painfully toward God's victory, which has already been signaled in Jesus Christ.

Yet, perception of God's ultimate authority in judgment over the affairs of this world is no guarantee that God's final verdict is at hand. Christians may know with certainty that God's promised judgment will be ultimate and final, but we cannot and do not know when God will move to enact that judgment. What Christians can and do know is this: the world will not receive us or our message about Jesus Christ any differently from the way the world received our Lord. The only sure thing for Christians is that we may be called to suffer. Perhaps we should recognize that if we are not experiencing the kind of persecution about which Jesus spoke (suffering for Christ's sake, not merely having a bad time), then there is a distinct possibility that we are not being faithful. Taking the message of Christ and his will and work into the world will lead Christians into conflict with the forces of evil, and we may end up suffering as faithful servants of Christ.

Nevertheless, because Jesus Christ suffered, died, was buried, and was raised, he now stands by the grace of God in a position to sustain his disciples in faithful steadfastness, no matter what we are called to face. Ultimately the fate of Christians is in the hands of our Lord Jesus Christ, and he promises us that our lives and our faithfulness are dear to him.

Proper 28: The Celebration

As we approach the end of the Christian year all three lessons lead us to consider the end of all time and they present us with very different emotions and reactions. For Isaiah the prospect is idyllic; the strains of "My Blue Heaven" float above the roses twining round the cabin door. For Paul the prospect is not yet realized and idle anticipation will not do in the meantime because our life-style is a form of witness about the Coming One. For Luke, living in anticipation of the end will be a judgment on the values of the world around us, and that will inevitably bring us into conflict with those who hold those values.

The church has embraced one or the other of those interpretations at different times in its history with significant consequences for how Christians lived their lives in the present. Isaiah's vision can easily become Marx's "opiate of the people," the "pie in the sky when you die" attitude that tolerates any amount of suffering and injustice in the present because it will all be compensated for later

140

on. The monastic movement, in its more vigorous manifestations of the *ora et labora* (pray and work) theme, has been akin to Paul's ideal Thessalonian community. And various sects and utopian communties have been encouraged by Luke's description of the last days and the persecution that will accompany any departure from the norms of the larger society as they have sought to save themselves from what they perceived to be a crooked generation. It may be that the commentary about the Old Testament lesson is also appropriate to the other two. We are delivered from escapist fantasy and from a rigorous discipline that ends up graceless, as well as from a judgmental view of those around us that interprets every misfortune as God's direct intervention by our participation in worship.

Worship provides the perspective because it makes us dependent upon God to bring the new order into being and not upon our own actions or attitudes. In the liturgy the Reign of God is apprehended by faith and our lives are ordered by its priorities. We are set free to fantasize because the realities of this world cannot begin to describe the sublime reality of life with God, which we get a taste of in the liturgy. So we find ourselves talking and singing about golden streets and ivory palaces and slain lambs sitting on thrones and glassy seas. Was it fantasy when an African slave in Georgia experienced freedom while in church? Or was it more real than the physical bondage? The liturgy does impose a discipline upon us. We bring in the offertory the results of our work in the world, the results of our (preferrably) having cooperated with God in the care of the creation that is being made new. And liturgy itself is a discipline if it is done in community, because it is only through the practice of "decency and order" that the rights of all in the assembly are respected. Finally, the liturgy is counter-cultural; it pronounces judgment upon the values of the world as it orders time and tells stories and insists on God's priorities. The reality of God's reign breaking through in the liturgy subverts all other realities. Ask the Russian peasant who for seventy years waited patiently from week to week for the sacred doors to open and give her a glimpse into heaven.

Those congregations that have begun to use a sung response as part of the psalter reading may wonder what to do with Isaiah 12 since it doesn't appear with a response in most collections. One option is to use for the response "There shall be wells of salvation/From which with joy we will draw" to the first two lines of the tune to the gospel hymn, "There Shall be Showers of Blessing." The response should be sung before the psalm and then after the second, fourth, and sixth verses.

Proper Twenty-nine [Christ the King] Sunday Between November 20 and 26 Inclusive

Old Testament Texts

Jeremiah 23:1-6 contains both an oracle of judgment against Judah's rulers during the close of the monarchy period and an oracle of salvation about a future Davidic monarch. Luke 1:68-79 is the song of Zechariah, the father of John the Baptist, which he sang at the birth of his son.

The Lesson: *Jeremiah 23:1-6*

Taking Responsibility for Leadership

Setting. Jeremiah 23:1-6 occurs in a larger section of oracles that include at least chapters 21:1–24:10. The setting for this section is given in 21:1-2 and in 24:1. Chapter 21:1-2 places the oracles during the reign of Zedekiah, who reigned from 597–587 B.C.E., at a time when Israel is under siege by Nebuchadnezzer, king of Babylon. This siege most likely took place around 587 B.C.E., and it resulted in the second deportation of people from Judah to Babylon, which is usually considered the fall of the Kingdom of Judah and the beginning of the exilic period. Chapter 24:1 refers to the first deportation that occured in 597 B.C.E. and it states how Jeconiah, the son of Jehoiakim, king of Judah, together with the princes of Judah were taken away to Babylon. These seperate introductions underscore how the literature in 21:1–24:10 has not been arranged in a strickly chronological sequence, since Zedekiah's rule (referred to in 21:1) only followed the deportation that is described in 24:1. More important than chronology is the emphasis on siege warfare and the loss of the land. The referrence to kings and rulers and, more specifically, to their deportation provides an important context for interpreting Jeremiah 23:1-6, since the primary focus of this text is to convey judgment against rulers in the way that they have exercised power.

Structure. The larger structure of Jeremiah 21:1–24:10 sets the mood for interpreting the lectionary text. It begins in Jeremiah 21 with an account of Zedekiah requesting an oracle from the prophet Jeremiah concerning the Babylonian siege. Jeremiah answers with a negative oracle of judgment. He states that God is against both the king and the city and that no divine aid will be given. Jeremiah 22 extends the message of judgment by recounting how past kings did not execute power justly and that, as a consequence, God is abandoning Jerusalem. Within this chapter the specific Judaen monarchs, Shallum (v. 11 = Jehoahaz, who reigned for one year in 609 B.C.E.), Jehoiakim (v. 18, who reigned from 609–598 B.C.E.), and Coniah (v. 24 = Jehoiachin, who reigned from 598–597 B.C.E. and was departed in the first deportation of 597 B.C.E.). Thus the judgment oracles in Jeremiah 21–22 trace the last four kings of Judah:

> Jehoahaz (609 B.C.E.)
> Jehoiakim (609–598 B.C.E.)
> Jehoiachin (598–597 B.C.E.)
> Zedekiah (597–587 B.C.E.)

Jeremiah 23:1-6 provides a conclusion to the divine judgment of the last kings of Judah. It begins with a woe oracle aimed at all the shepherds (kings) who destroy the sheep in the pasture. The larger context provides reason for including vv. 7-8 within the unit. The criticism of the prophet in Jeremiah 21:1–24:10 includes not only the leadership of kings but also the leadership of prophets. The oracles directed at kings extends from 21:1 through 23:8, with judgment oracles against prophets commencing in 23:9-40. The conclusion to the judgment oracles against kings in Jeremiah 23:1-8 can be outlined in the following manner.

> I. Woe Oracle against the shepherds (v. 1)
> II. Divine Accusation and Judgment (v. 2)

III. A Return to the Land for the Remnant (vv. 3-4)
IV. The Promise of a Davidic King (vv. 5-6)
V. A New Exodus (vv. 7-8)

Significance. The most notable aspect of Jeremiah 23:1-6 (7-8) for Christians is the promise of a future king in vv. 5-6, which has taken on a long and rich interpretative life as a messianic prophecy about Jesus. In fact this imagery may be reflected in the psalm response of Luke 1:68-79. But such a quick messianic interpretation does not go to the heart of Jeremiah 23:1-6 (7-8). This text is not governed by the messianic promise at the end of the passage (vv. 5-6) but by the woe oracle at the beginning (v. 1). The central features of the lectionary text are a lament and divine judgment on the abuse of power by leaders within the community of faith and the disastrous consequences that such abuse unleashes on the people of God. For ancient Israel this will mean nothing less than the loss of the promised land.

The abuse of power is spelled out clearly in the text; it is not tending to the sheep. The prophet makes this explicit through the imagery of destroying, scattering, driving away, and not attending to the needs of the sheep as accusations against past and present shepherds. Yet the judgment oracles also raise the question of whether there are any guidelines within the text that might bring us beyond judgment and perhaps outline what the proper exercise of power might be among leaders? And, in seeking an answer to this question, it is the vision of a future monarch in vv. 5-6 that provides the guidelines. Here the prophet states that a genuine exercise of power within the community of faith requires that the king (or any leader) embody the qualities of righteousness and justice to the point where his name becomes, "The Lord is our righteousness." In Hebrew this is very similar to the name Zedekiah, which raises questions about the relationship of this oracle of salvation and the exiled king, Zedekiah. Does the prophet hope for his return or is the vision of a good king meant to be yet another form of judgment on the exiled king? Whatever the relationship may be, it is clear that the qualities of leadership described in vv. 5-6 are not meant to be a utopian messianic vision but practical quidelines on how power is exercised by leaders in the here and now. And it is from this perspective that Jeremiah 23:1-6 (7-8) should be preached. Such a practical text can certainly provide helpful guidelines for leaders who exercise power in any local church. The exercise of righteousness for the good of the community may provide insight into the way in which Jesus embodied divine power.

The Response: *Luke 1:68-79*

A Hymn of Praise or a Prophecy of Judgment?

Setting. Luke used hymns throughout the opening chapters of his Gospel to provide commentary on the events of Mary's conception (the Magnificat), the birth of John the Baptist (the Benedictus stated by Zechariah, the father of John), and the presentation of Jesus in the temple (the Nunc Dimittis by Simeon). One reason why the Benedictus is providing a response to the Old Testament lesson is that Jeremiah 23:5-6 is referred to in Luke 1:7, where John the Baptist is interpreted as being the messenger, who will prepare the way for the Lord.

Structure. Luke 1:68-79 can be separated into two or three parts. Verses 68-75 are a hymn of praise, while vv. 76-79 are more prophetic in tone, for Zechariah is pictured addressing John directly. One could break the structure into three parts by limiting the prophetic discourse to vv. 76-77, with the result that vv. 78-79 provide a summary and a conclusion to the song.

Significance. The Benedictus is not the language of leaders, which was the focus in Jeremiah 23:1-6 (7-8), but the language of faith from those who are scattered and eagerly anticipating the renewed salvation of God.

New Testament Texts

The language of Kingdom in the verses from Colossians and the lofty words of praise for God's Son suggest the appropriateness of this portion of Colossians for Proper Twenty-nine, also called Christ the King or Reign of Christ Sunday. Similarly the dramatic portion of the story of Christ's crucifixion from the Gospel according to Luke records the words of the inscription set over Jesus' head as he hung on the cross, "This is the King of the Jews."

146

The Epistle: *Colossians 1:11-20*

The Glories of the Kingdom of God's Son

Setting. In geographical terms Colossae was the least significant city to which one of the thirteen canonical letters attributed to Paul was written. In the mid-first century this former city had declined into a small town, which was destroyed by an earthquake in 63 C.E. and apparently never rebuilt. The letter itself indicates that the Colossians were enamored or were in danger of being enamored of a strange syncretistic religio-philosophy based on wisdom speculation. Colossians 2:8 refers to the "philosophy" and 2:23 makes clear the ascetic tendency of the thought and practice. In turn, 2:18 shows that somehow, someone thought and taught that through self-abasement the Colossians could experience "the worship of the angels"—most likely meaning "to join the angels in worship." Moreover, the practice of achieving ecstasy through self-denial had been mixed with the teachings of Christianity. The letter seeks to correct and to clarify the situation, primarily through robust christological teaching.

Structure. Colossians combines large sections of theological and ethical instruction. At times one wonders whether a statement is doctrinal or practical, or both. The reading for this Sunday comes from the letter's body (1:9–3:17), which is the most doctrinal section of the epistle. Verse 11 is a part of vv. 9-11 which are themselves a coherent unit of thought, despite the versification and paragraphing of the NRSV. In Greek the words translated "while joyfully" at the end of verse 11 are literally "with joy" and should be read with the first words of v. 12 as a new sentence—"With joy giving thanks. . . ." In turn, v. 12 begins a call to give thanks to God for what God had done for believers in God's Son; this call runs through v. 14. Next, vv. 15-20 offer the lines of what scholars widely regard as an early Christian hymn. Thus we have (1) a prayerful wish for the strengthening of the Colossians (v. 11); (2) a call to thanksgiving for redemption (vv. 12-14); and (3) poetic praise of God's Son. The content of the final section of praise is remarkable.

Significance. The initial line of the reading informs us that we may, because of God's gracious power, give thanks to God for the gift of our redemption, which is forgiveness of sins. Furthermore, we are reminded that our redemption was made real by God's work in and through his Son, Jesus Christ (who is not named here).

In vv. 12-20 the focus shifts to a give a grand christological confession, including the call to thanksgiving and the lofty praise of God's Son. The language of "inheritance" and the "Kingdom" points beyond the blessing the Colossians have and are experiencing in the past and present to the full form of God's promised, future glory. The hymn in vv. 15-20 is an early Christian liturgical piece that declares the ultimate quality of Christ and his supremacy over all other powers. With few exceptions, interpreters understand that, here, Christ is confessed as being pre-existent. Yet, even in this lofty praise Christ's pre-existence is not a passive being alongside God; rather, one finds that Christ is active as the Head of the Cosmos. The hymn focuses on Christ in two distinguishable but related movements: As Christ was active in creation, even so, now he is active as the Head of a new divinely created corporate entity—namely, the body of Christ which is the church.

The composition of the church according to these verses is quite striking, for it is made up of "all things, whether on earth or in heaven" that are reconciled in and through Christ himself. This cosmic view of reconciliation is a majestic statement of the magnitude of the saving work of Jesus Christ, and the preacher should be encouraged to declare boldly the wonder of Christ's accomplishment. The poetic, imaginative language is not our normal, more prosaic manner of expressing the meaning of God's work in Jesus Christ, so that frequently we shy away from proclaiming the marvel of redemption because of our own lack of an adequate, contemporary vocabulary and metaphor for declaring the wonder of God's work.

We may find stimulation for thinking about the meaning of this text for today if we notice that, on the one hand, the hymn proclaims Christ as the Head of Creation and the Head of the Church and, on the other hand, the hymn is informed by many unstated assumptions. Something that is not stated in this hymn happened after Christ acted to create all things in heaven and on earth. Somehow death entered the picture; there came to be a lack of peace; and a need for reconciliation came to be. In this situation the hymn celebrates Christ the head of creation acting as Christ the agent of cosmic redemption. The hymn praises Christ the head of the church who achieved victory over death, brought peace, and accomplished reconciliation. We should see that the hymn does not describe the problem; rather it declares and celebrates the solution.

The Gospel: *Luke 23:33-43*

Christ the King Who Saves

Setting. The discussion of setting for the Gospel lesson for Proper Twenty-seven gives general information concerning the verses of this lesson. As a whole, Luke's account of the Passion is styled to indicate the eschatological significance of the time. Moreover, we learn that Jesus knows and makes provision for the faithfulness of his followers. And, in addition, we see that Jesus' Passion was faithful obedience to the will of God which brings the salvation of humanity.

Structure. Two scenes from the Passion narrative make up our lesson. First, vv. 32-38 recount the scene at the cross. The material is dramatically arranged with characters coming and going, speaking in telling words as they appear. In the midst of the insults, Jesus' memorable prayer in v. 34 tells the truth of God's merciful work in relation to human depravity. Second, vv. 39-43 tell the story of Jesus and the two criminals who were crucified at Jesus' right and left. Both scenes demonstrate the abundant mercy of Christ the King.

Significance. Luke penned this account in blunt prose, showing neither an interest in presenting the gory details of the crucifixion, nor the glory of righteous suffering. The telling of the events of the crucifixion is reserved, so that Jesus' own mercy contrasts sharply with the insulting acts and hostile words of those around him at the time of his dying. Verse 34*a* is a problem, because many ancient and reliable manuscripts simply do not contain the words of Jesus' prayer. Thus, in the NRSV the first portion of this verse appears in double-brackets to indicate the uncertainty of the editors of the translation concerning the authenticity of the line. Nevertheless, the recent tendency in scholarship is to accept the words of Jesus' prayer as a part of Luke's original text. Interpreters increasingly argue the prayer would have been deleted at a later time in the life of the church when anti-Jewish sentiment was high and when scribes could not accept that Christ had prayed for the forgiveness of the Jews who rejected him. The language, theology, and disposition of the prayer are fully compatible with Jesus as we know him from the rest of Luke's Gospel.

The events Luke recalls are told so as to emphasize that Jesus' death was the fulfillment of prophecy—his own, as we know it from the Gospel, and that of the Old Testament. First, the soldiers cast lots for Jesus' garments; thus, "fulfilling" Psalm 22. Second, the religious rulers scoffed the crucified Jesus; again, "fulfilling" Psalm 22 and reflecting an interest in Wisdom 2:17-24. The religious leaders mocked Jesus with appropriate religious language, "the Christ of God, his holy one," implying ironically (as we the readers see) that Jesus was not the Christ. Third, the soldiers mocked Jesus by offering him vinegar (soured, cheap wine); so that their gestures "fulfilled" Psalm 69. The soldiers, however, employ political language in their insults, calling Jesus "the King of the Jews." They too speak so that the readers of this story see the deep irony of their taunts, for Christian faith perceives that indeed the crucified Jesus was the King of the Jews. Moreover, in the insults of both the religious leaders and the soldiers we find the implication that Jesus could not save himself. The gospel truth is that by not simply saving himself, Jesus saved humankind. By not merely looking out for himself, Jesus rendered the greatest imaginable service for others.

In the ensuing scene still another mocker, one of the criminals, derides Jesus as a false messiah—again, implying that Jesus does not have the power to save. Thus, for a third time Jesus' power to save is called into question. As the story continues, in the exchange between Jesus and the penitent criminal who defended Jesus against the other criminal's insults, we see clearly Jesus' power to save in the promise of salvation to the penitent brigand. Strikingly, the penitent criminal turned to Jesus as the Coming King, and in his words he actually expressed the Christian hope of Christ's coming in power.

In his sheer equanimity, Jesus is the Lord of this scene. As we see him crucified, Luke remembers how he died sure of his fate and with the power to promise salvation to another. Above all, we learn that Christ the King has the power to save.

Proper 29: The Celebration

"Lord Jesus, Think on Me," a hymn by Synesius of Cyrene, a late fourth-century Greek poet, is based upon the plea of the penitent thief to Christ in today's Gospel, and it has made its appearance in several recent hymnals—*Hymnal: A Worship Book* (Brethren and Mennonite), no. 527; *The Hymnal 1982* (Episcopal), no. 641; *The Lutheran Book of Worship*, no. 309; and *The Presbyterian Hymnal*, no. 301. It may be used after the prayer of confession and before the declaration of pardon or as the hymn between the Gospel reading and the sermon. The Taize petition, "Jesus, Remember Me," may be used as a prayer response or as a preparation for the intercessions and petitions. In the latter case it should be repeated several times as an aid in centering upon the task at hand. Of the books mentioned previously, it can be found in the Brethren (no. 247) and Presbyterian (no. 599) books. It is also in *The United Methodist Hymnal* (no. 488).

The Canticle of Zechariah appears in metrical form in the following hymnals: United Methodist, no. 209; Presbyterian, no. 602; Brethren, no. 174; Southern Baptist, no. 79; and Episcopal, no. 444. It is also in *Worship: A Hymnal and Service Book for Roman Catholics* (Chicago: GIA, 1986), no. 6.

It should be observed for those unaware of it that the Canticle of Zechariah, the Benedictus, is the appointed canticle for Morning Prayer in the monastic tradition of the West. This means that the church daily proclaims what we proclaim today as a kind of summary statement on this last Sunday of the Christian year that "he has come to his people and set them free" (*The Book of Common Prayer,* p. 92). Here is a magnificent declaration and reminder of what God has done in our lives through the life, death, and resurrection of Jesus Christ. It is not the expression of a wishful hope that things might get better, but it is an audacious affirmation that things have not been the same since that intervention in history. And it is a daily reminder to us who use it devotionally that we have been enlisted as latter-day John the Baptists to prepare the way for others. It is both celebration and commission, designed to help us see the new day in a new light. On this Sunday of Christ the King, it can help us see the new year in a new light as we offer it to the One who has "rescued us from the power of darkness" (Col. 13*a*).

Worship leaders should be careful when choosing hymns for today to be certain that any use of the term *King* refers to the Second Person of the Trinity and not the First!

A regretable loss in many recent hymnals is that from the Baptist tradition, "Majestic Sweetness Sits Enthroned." Its images are particularly fitted to today's lessons. Since both text and tune are in public domain, it might be reproduced for church bulletins. Another loss is "How Sweet the Name of Jesus Sounds." One of its stanzas, altered and sung to St. Peter, would be especially appropriate today at the presentation of the offering:

> Jesus, our Savior, shepherd, friend,
> our prophet, priest, and king,
> our Lord, our life, our way, our end,
> accept the gifts we bring.

Thanksgiving Day

Old Testament Texts

Deuteronomy 26:1-11 provides cultic instructions for the offering of first fruits. Psalm 100 is a processional hymn.

The Lesson: *Deuteronomy 26:1-11*

The Power of Giving

Setting. Deuteronomy 26:1-11 is a liturgical text that describes in detail how the offering of first fruits must be carried out. The text presupposes a theology of sacrifice. A brief summary of what it means to give within the setting of sacrifice will provide background for interpreting the offering of first fruits. G. Van der Leeuw in his classic study *Religion in Essence and Manifestation* underscores how "giving" within sacrifice is essentially three things: it is personal, it creates communion, and it is reciprocal. First, by stating that giving in sacrifice is personal, Van der Leeuw means that the gift is never simply an object of which one is unilaterally disposing, but actually part of one's self. Second, since the gift is in fact personal (part of one's self) it creates a bond between the giver and the recipient. Thus the gift creates communion because it is an attempt to place one's self in relation to another by means of an object. The central point here is to see that the gift is the central force that creates communion (not the giver or the receiver), since by participating in it both the giver and the receiver are bonded to each other. The communal nature of the sacrificial gift leads to the third conclusion—namely, that the giving of gifts is inherently reciprocal, since both giver and receiver participate in the gift. Van der Leeuw describes the reciprocal nature of sacrificial gifts in the following manner: "Giving demands a gift . . . because the gift allows a stream to flow," which from the moment of giving runs uninterruptedly from donor to recipient and from receiver to giver: "the recipient is in the power of the giver." The gift of the first fruits in Deuteronomy 26:1-11 illustrates these three points.

Structure. Deuteronomy 26:1-11 consists of liturgical instructions that separate into three parts. Verse 1 is essential for interpreting the larger passage, for it provides the setting that is prompting the sacrificial instructions in the first place.

Once Israel has entered the land then the following ritual practice of first fruits must be performed:

   I. The first ritual action and confession (vv. 2-3)
        Ritual action (vv. 2-3*a*)
           "Take first fruits . . ."
           "Place [it] in a basket . . ."
           "Go to the place [sanctuary] . . ."
           "Go to the priest . . ."
        Confession (vv. 3*b*)
           Affirmation of being in the land
  II. The second ritual action and confession (vv. 4-10)
        Ritual action (v. 4)
           The priest will take the basket . . . place it before God . . .
        Confession (vv. 5-10)
          A recounting of salvation history in three parts:
            Events leading to Egyptian oppression
            Events involved in the exodus
            Present situation in the land
 III. The third ritual action (v. 11)
        Worship and communal celebration

Significance. The focus of this text is neither on God nor Israel, but on the land. The land is the gift and hence the central force that creates a bond between God and Israel. The first task of interpretation is to determine whose gift is the land. Verse 1 answers this question unequivocally. The land is God's gift to Israel. God's ownership of the land and his subsequent gift of it to Israel is the religious basis for the offering of first fruits. The sacrifice is rooted in the confession that the produce of the land, especially the first-ripe fruits, is God's property, which means that it is holy and should be transferred to God. But the harvest is also the product of Israel, and this empirical fact provides the starting point for the ritual instructions.

Three conclusions follow at this point. First, the offering of first fruits is personal. This is particularly evident in the two confessions that the worshiper is instructed to recite during the liturgical events. These confessions go beyond the simple transfer of the first fruits back to God to include statements about the status of the worshiper in relation to God. In v. 4 the worshiper acknowledges (1) being present in the land and (2) that the offering of first fruits is a sign that God has fulfilled the divine promises of salvation. The historical credo in vv. 5-10 supports the first confession by providing an elaboration of the process by which God brought Israel into the land.

Second, the confessions also underscore how the sacrifice creates communion between God and the worshiper. Here we see that the very act of offering first fruits is meant to articulate the relationship between God and Israel that is described briefly in the historical credo. This relationship is rooted in divine promise (v. 3, "the land that the LORD swore to our ancestors to give us."), and it is God's fulfilling of his obligations that is making the ritual possible.

Third, the offering of first fruits is reciprocal, so much in fact that it is impossible to decide who is the giver and who is the receiver. If we start at v. 1, with the notice of how God gave Israel the land, then God is the giver and Israel receives the gift through the produce of the land. It then follows that in the offering of first fruit Israel is the receiver giving back the gift. If, however, we start at v. 2, then Israel is the giver and God is the recipient, who returns the gift to the worshiper (v. 11) in the form ot the communal feast. This never ending circle in which the gift of the land is given and received over and over is the primary metaphor of salvation in the book of Deuteronomy, and it gives rise to an ethic, which Van der Leeuw would state in the following way: "I give in order that thou mayest be able to give." When framed in this way, one must expect a blessing from God when giving the divine a gift, not because it is economically in the self-interest of the worshiper, but simply because that is the way of salvation. The passing back and forth of gifts creates a bond between God and the people of God, with the result that in the end, "the principle feature (of giving) is not that someone or other should receive something, but that the stream of life should continue to flow" (Van der Leeuw, p. 351)

The Response: *Psalm 100*

A Processional Hymn

Setting. Verse 4 provides a strong indication that Psalm 100 functioned as a processional hymn in Israelite worship. The call for the worshiper to enter God's gate and then to proceed into the divine court suggests that the hymn was used outside of the Temple, and that it signaled the start of worship.

Structure. Psalm 100 consists of two introits. Verses 1-3 and 4-5 each function as a call to worship. Verse 1 summons the all of the earth to praise God, while v. 4 narrows the focus down to those who are about to enter the sanctuary.

Significance. Two reasons are given for praising God in Psalm 100. God is worthy of praise in vv. 1-3 because he is the Creator. Verse 3 summons those outside the Temple to praise God because "he made us and we are his." Verses 4-5 provide more content to the relationship between Creator and humans by exploring the salvific character of God. "The Lord is good" and "his steadfast love endures."

New Testament Texts

In Philippians Paul offers practical spiritual advice, and his charge to "rejoice" makes this passage especially appropriate for Thanksgiving worship. Combined with the exhortation to rejoice are words of assurance about God's care, a declaration of divine peace, and a call to continue living a life that is pleasing to God. The themes are all suggestive for Thanksgiving proclamation. The lesson from John is the opening portion of Jesus' beautiful, but difficult, discourse on the Bread of Life. The idea of feeding on Jesus may provide a bridge for meditation on Thanksgiving.

The Epistle: *Philippians 4:4-9*

The Shape and Substance of Life in Christ

Setting. Much of Paul's essentially friendly letter to the Philippians is practical in nature. Throughout the epistle he offers the congregation helpful advice about their life in Christ (for example, see 1:27–2:18 and 3:2-21). Nevertheless, the verses of the reading are even more pointedly practical. In this passage Paul moves from the level of general, helpful remarks to give specific instructions about particular issues in the life of the congregation. The call to godly living in v. 9 is rooted in the assurance that God is with the believers in all of life.

Structure. The reading occurs in the midst of several relatively independent pieces of advice that are brought together in 4:1-9. This larger section opens with the word *therefore* (4:1), which demonstrates that all that will follow is related to Paul's explicit admonitions in the previous verses (3:14, 21). There he told the Philippians to press on toward the goal of "the heavenly call of God in Christ Jesus" with full confidence in Jesus Christ, who has "the power . . . to make all things subject to himself." In this context, Paul twice states a command to "rejoice" (v. 4) and, then, continues with further pieces of "spiritual" advice in vv. 5-7. Verses 8-9 begin to bring the letter to its conclusion.

Significance. It is crucial to recognize that the basis of the instructions that Paul issues in these verses. The opening word of v. 1, *therefore,* sets the apostle's directions on the foundation of the preceding words of encouragement in 3:12-21, especially vv. 15-21. The power to accomplish what Paul instructs the Philippians to do is not simply their own efforts and energies; rather they live and work together in the context of the power of the Lord Jesus Christ, who as the Savior will transform the Philippians into his own likeness. Seldom does so much of Paul's deep affection for a congregation come through in his remarks as it does in 4:1. Yet, even this is not mere fondness, but genuine Christian devotion as is clear from Paul's use of the phrase, "in the Lord."

Verses 4-9 move to a lofty level of reflection and direction as Paul describes the activities and characteristics of Christian life: rejoic-

157

ing, gentleness, lack of anxiety, prayer, thanksgiving, purity of life, and peace. Consultation of serious commentaries and a good theological dictionary will reward those who wish to develop these words into themes for preaching. Yet, other approaches to the passage are possible. To illustrate, notice in these statements the context of Christian life: "in the Lord" (4:4); the motivation of this life: "the Lord is near" (4:5); the orientation of such a life: "to God" (4:6); the source of such a life: "of God" (4:7); and the power for such a life: "the God of peace will be with you." Thus, while the characteristics listed above are suggestive for preaching, perhaps a fuller treatment of this text will deal with "Christian Life: Its Characteristics, Context, Motivation, Orientation, Source, and Assurance." For Thanksgiving proclamation, a stress on the "source" and "assurance" may prove beneficial. From start to finish, the preacher should remember, and in the preaching remind the congregation, that Christian life is not lived as a job to be performed, but as a privilege to be experienced in relation to the person and the power of the Lord Jesus Christ. Far from telling the Philippians merely to relax and enjoy living, Paul directs them to an active life of faith that is anxiety-free because of the presence and power of the Lord. The thanks that Christians give comes from the certitude for living in relation to our Lord.

The Gospel: *John 6:25-35*

Jesus Christ, the Bread of Life

Setting. Much of this chapter of John is remarkably similar in subject and sequence to portions of Mark 6 and 8; so that many interpreters suggest a very primitive early Christian story-cycle lies behind the Gospels' versions of these events. But unlike the other stories (feeding the five thousand and walking on the water) there is no parallel to our lesson in the other Gospels.

Structure. Interpreters suggest a variety of structures for the verses of our lesson, but the dominant perspective seems to be as follows: (1) Verse 25 is part of a larger report in vv. 22-25 about the curiosity of the crowd on finding Jesus on the other side of the sea despite his not having access to a boat for crossing. The people finally put a question to Jesus. And, (2) this query sets up the ensuing dialogue (vv. 26-34 or 35) which leads into the extensive "bread of life" discourse (vv. 35 or 36-59). Notice in the exchange between Jesus and the people in vv. 26-35 that Jesus confronts the people and makes revelatory declarations about himself rather than answers the question. In the discussion of significance we presuppose the crowd's curiosity and move to treat the dialogue (vv. 26-34) and Jesus' bold declaration (v. 35).

Significance. In the unconventional logic of the Gospel according to John, the question of the crowd, which seems never to be answered, may mean far more than "How did you get across the lake?" Jesus certainly does not answer that simple question, but instead, he takes on the crowd and ends up making metaphorical, revelatory declarations about his true origin and identity.

The text is packed with significant terms and phrases, for example, "signs," "eternal life," "Son of Man," "[God's] seal," "the works of God," "believe," "sent," "the (true) bread from heaven," "comes down from heaven," and "life." These are uttered knowingly by Jesus and heard in seeming ignorance by those with whom he speaks. The text works with a common Johannine literary technique, wherein the conversation possesses two levels of meaning. Jesus talks in metaphors about divine truths and wonders, but the people hear and think in earth-bound terms that preclude their understanding. As readers of this Gospel we stand in a privileged position between Jesus and the people, knowing far less than Jesus who teaches us, but far more than the people who never seem to have a clue about their ignorance or Jesus' meanings.

As an inventory of the terminology in these verses reveals, this passage, like most others in John, contains the whole gospel in a nutshell. If we will allow ourselves to stand with the people, but with the capacity to hear and understand Jesus, then this lesson imparts a profound message indeed.

Like the people we wonder about Jesus—Who is he? Where did he come from? What is he doing here? As he replies in his strange Johannine voice he tells us these things and more. We have a tendency to come to Jesus for the wrong reasons, most often to get something from him which is far less than he is prepared and willing to give. In our small-mindedness we thwart the riches of God's grace. Our limited perspective gives us little expectations. We give our lives to achieving ends that are temporal, ephemeral; perhaps seeking the good, we never come to know the better and the best. Or, if we know the better (Moses' manna), we may be so content with it that we never experience the exhilarating freedom of faith in Christ.

Jesus Christ comes to us as the grace of God, calling us beyond of our limited perspective and out of our limited patterns of living. God's gift to us is a transforming relationship to Jesus Christ who empowers us to live into a fullness of life, which is God's real intention for our living. If we can come through our encounter with this text to the point that we simply raise our level of expectations, then we have heard what the passage is saying in these verses. The text simply provokes greater expectations. Other crucial questions will naturally follow from perceiving the basic point that in Jesus Christ God is calling us beyond the current limits of our living to a new and vital life oriented toward "eternal life" and "the works of God." Naturally, we wonder what such a life looks like, but the scope of our lesson may require us to put this kind of question on hold, for we learn in other passages what it means never to hunger or thirst because of our belief in Jesus Christ.

Thanksgiving: The Celebration

The Old Testament commentary above about the ongoing reciprocity between God and Israel calls to mind Psalm 116:12-13 where the psalmist asks, "What shall I return to the LORD/for all his bounty to me?" and then answers the question immediately by declaring, "I will lift up the cup of salvation/and call on the name of the LORD." In other words, the psalmist is returning what has been first given and then in calling on the Lord's name will once more receive salvation. Charles Wesley has paraphrased this in a hymn that would be particularly fitting as the offertory hymn on this Thanksgiving Day because it can provide a connection between the offertory theme of the Old Testament lesson, the exhortation to rejoice in the epistle reading, and the eucharistic implications of the

Gospel lesson. It has most recently been sung to "Armenia," but other common meter tunes can be used.

1. What shall I render to my God
   for all his mercy's store?
   I'll take the gifts he hath bestowed,
   and humbly ask for more.

2. The sacred cup of saving grace
   I will with thanks receive,
   and all his promises embrace,
   and to his glory live.

3. My vows I will to his great name
   before his people pay,
   and all I have, and all I am,
   upon his altar lay.

4. The God of all-redeeming grace
   my God I will proclaim,
   offer the sacrifice of praise,
   and call upon his name.

5. Praise God, ye saints, the God of love
   who hath my sins forgiven,
   till, gathered to the Church above,
   we sing the songs of heaven.

Psalm 100 is popularly known in metrical versions as "All People That on Earth Do Dwell" and "Before Jehovah's Awe-ful Throne," and so has given its name, "Old Hundreth," to the tune used with those texts and which we usually associate with the Doxology.

Thanksgiving can be a time to incorporate into the service with greater intention liturgical elements that deal with the sacredness of creation and our place in it and responsibility towards it. Some suggestions for background materials and liturgical resources were listed in this volume under the Celebration entry for Proper Nineteen.

Preachers who are struggling with the tension implicit in the popular expectation that the day is an exercise in patriotism over against what they understand as the demands of the Gospel may be helped by paying careful attention to the Gospel lesson. The crowd felt confident of God's care because their ancestors had been provided for in the past. Jesus warned them against any attitude that judges political success purely on its ability to provide bread. Success for the Christian is measured in terms of those attitudes that Paul lists in the epistle reading and that come from trust in God.

The traditional benediction that begins, "The peace of God which passes all understanding" is based on Philippians 4:7. Verse 8 may be used as the final charge to the congregation and v. 7 could then begin the formal benediction or blessing.

Scripture Index

Old Testament

New Testament

A Comparison of Major Lectionaries

YEAR C: PROPERS 17 THROUGH 29 AND ALL SAINTS AND THANKSGIVING DAYS

	Old Testament	Psalm	Epistle	Gospel
PROPER 17 (August 28—September 3)				
[RC: 22nd Ordinary Time]			[Luth: Pentecost 15]	
RCL	Jer. 2:4-13	81:1, 10-16	Heb. 13:1-8, 15-16	Luke 14:1, 7-14
RoCath	Sir. 3:17-18, 20, 28-29	68:4-7, 10-11	Heb. 12:18-19, 22-24	
Episcopal	Sir. 10:(7-11) 12-18	112	Heb. 13:1-8	
Lutheran	Prov. 25:6-7	112	Heb. 13:1-8	
PROPER 18 (September 4-10)				
[RC: 23rd Ordinary Time]			[Luth: Pentecost 16]	
RCL	Jer. 18:1-11	139:1-6, 13-18	Philemon 1-21	Luke 14:25-33
RoCath	Wis. 9:13-18	90:3-6, 12-17	Philemon 9-10, 12-17	
Episcopal	Deut. 30:15-20	1	Philemon 1-20	
Lutheran	Prov. 9:8-12	10:12-15, 17-19	Philemon 1 (2-9) 10-21	

PROPER 19 (September 11-17)
[RC: 24th Ordinary Time]   [Luth: Pentecost 17.]

RCL	Jer. 4:11-12, 22-28	14		Luke 15:1-10
RoCath	Exod. 32:7-11, 13-14	51:3-4, 12-13, 17, 19	I Tim. 1:12-17	Luke 15:1-10 (11-32)
Episcopal	Exod. 32:1, 7-14	51:1-18		
Lutheran	Exod. 32:7-14	51:1-18		

PROPER 20 (September 18-24)
[RC: 25th Ordinary Time]   [Luth: Pentecost 18]

RCL	Jer. 8:18–9:1	79:1-9	I Tim. 2:1-7	Luke 16:1-13
RoCath	Amos 8:4-7	113:1-2, 4-8	I Tim. 2:1-8	
Episcopal	Amos 8:4-7 (8-12)	138	I Tim. 2:1-8	
Lutheran	Amos 8:4-7	113	I Tim. 2:1-8	

PROPER 21 (September 25–October 1)
[RC: 26th Ordinary Time]   [Luth: Pentecost 19]

RCL	Jer. 32:1-3a, 6-15	91:1-6, 14-16	I Tim. 6:6-19	Luke 16:19-31
RoCath	Amos 6:1, 4-7	146:7-10	I Tim. 6:11-16	
Episcopal	Amos 6:1-7	146	I Tim. 6:11-19	
Lutheran	Amos 6:1-7	146	I Tim. 6:6-16	

PROPER 22 (October 2-8)
[RC: 27th Ordinary Time]   [Luth: Pentecost 20]

RCL	Lam. 1:1-6	137	II Tim. 1:1-14	Luke 17:5-10
RoCath	Hab. 1:2-3; 2:2-4	95:1-2, 6-9	II Tim. 1:6-8, 13-14	
Episcopal	Hab. 1:1-13; 2:1-4	37:1-18		
Lutheran	Hab. 1:1-3; 2:1-4			

PROPER 23 (October 9-15)
[RC: 28th Ordinary Time]   [Luth: Pentecost 21]

RCL	Jer. 29:1, 4-7	66:1-12	II Tim. 2:8-15	Luke 17:11-19
RoCath	II Kings 5:14-17	98:1-4	II Tim. 2:8-13	
Episcopal	Ruth 1:(1-7) 8-19a	113	II Tim. 2:(3-7) 8-15	
Lutheran	Ruth 1:1-19a	111	II Tim. 2:8-13	

PROPER 24 (October 16-22)
[RC: 29th Ordinary Time]   [Luth: Pentecost 22]

RCL	Jer. 31:27-34	119:97-104	II Tim. 3:14–4:5	Luke 18:1-8
RoCath	Exod. 17:8-13	121	II Tim. 3:14–4:2	
Episcopal	Gen. 32:3-8, 22-30	121		Luke 18:1-8a
Lutheran	Gen. 32:22-30	121		Luke 18;1-8a

PROPER 25 (October 23-29)
[RC: 30th Ordinary Time]   [Luth: Pentecost 23]

RCL	Joel 2:23-32	65	II Tim. 4:6-8, 16-18	Luke 18:9-14
RoCath	Sirach 35:12-14, 16-18	34:2-3, 17-19		
Episcopal	Jer. 14:(1-6) 7-10, 19-22	84		
Lutheran	Deut. 10:12-22	34		

PROPER 26 (October 30–November 5)
[RC: 31st Ordinary Time]   [Luth: Pentecost 24]

RCL	Hab. 1:1-4; 2:1-4	119:137-44	II Thess. 1:1-4, 11-12	Luke 19:1-10
RoCath	Wisdom 11:22–12:1	145:1-2, 8-11, 13-14	II Thess. 1:11–2:2	
Episcopal	Isa. 1:10-20	32	II Thess. 1:1-5 (6-10) 11-12	
Lutheran	Exod. 34:5-9	145	II Thess. 1:1-5, 11-12	

PROPER 27 (November 6-12)
[RC: 32nd Ordinary Time]   [Luth: Pentecost 24]

RCL	Hag. 1:15b–2:9	145:1-5, 17-21	II Thess. 2:1-5, 13-17	Luke 20:27-38
RoCath	II Mac. 7:1-2, 9-14	17:1, 5-6, 8, 15	II Thess. 2:16–3:5	
Episcopal	Job 19:23-27a	17	II Thess. 2:13–3:5	
Lutheran	I Chron. 29:10-13	148	II Thess. 2:13–3:5	

PROPER 28 (November 13-19)
[RC: 33rd Ordinary Time]   [Luth: Pentecost 26]

RCL	Isa. 65:17-25	Isa. 12	II Thess. 3:6-13	Luke 21:5-19
RoCath	Mal. 3:19-20	98:5-9	II Thess. 3:7-12	
Episcopal	Mal. 3:13–4:2a, 5-6	98		
Lutheran	Mal. 4:1-2a	98		

PROPER 29 (November 20-26)
[RC: Last in Ordinary Time]   [Luth: Last after Pentecost]

RCL	Jer. 23:1-6	Luke 1:68-79	Col. 1:11-20	Luke 23:33-43
RoCath	II Sam. 5:1-3	122:1-5	Col. 1:12-20	Luke 23:35-43
Episcopal		46		Luke 23:35-43
Lutheran	Jer. 23:2-6	95:1-7a	Col. 1:13-20	Luke 23:35-43

ALL SAINTS DAY (Nov. 1 or the Sunday following)
[RC: 30th Ordinary Time]   [Luth: Pentecost 23]

RCL	Dan. 7:1-3, 15-18	149	Eph. 1:11-23	Luke 6:20-31
RoCath	Rev. 7:2-4, 9-14	24:1-6	I John 3:1-3	Matt. 5:1-12
Episcopal	Sir. 2:(1-6) 7-11			Luke 6:20-26 (27-36)
Lutheran	Isa. 26:1-4, 8-9, 12-13, 19-21	34:1-10	Rev. 21:9-11, 22-27 (22:1-5)	Matt. 5:1-12

THANKSGIVING DAY

RCL	Deut. 26:1-11	100	Phil. 4:4-9	John 6:25-35
RoCath	Sir. 50:22-24 or Zeph. 3:14-15	145:2-11	I Cor. 1:3-9	Luke 17:11-19
Episcopal	Deut. 8:1-3, 6-10 (17-20)	65	James 1:17-18, 21-27	Matt. 6:25-33
Lutheran	Deut. 8:1-10	65	Phil. 4:6-20	Luke 17:11-19

171

A Liturgical Calendar

September Through Christ the King 1993–2001

	1993 A	1994 B	1995 C	1996 A	1997 B
Proper 17	Aug. 29	Aug. 28	Sept. 3	Sept. 1	Aug. 31
Proper 18	Sept. 5	Sept. 4	Sept. 10	Sept. 8	Sept. 7
Proper 19	Sept. 12	Sept. 11	Sept. 17	Sept. 15	Sept. 14
Proper 20	Sept. 19	Sept. 18	Sept. 24	Sept. 22	Sept. 21
Proper 21	Sept. 26	Sept. 25	Oct. 1	Sept. 29	Sept. 28
Proper 22	Oct. 3	Oct. 2	Oct. 8	Oct. 6	Oct. 5
Proper 23	Oct. 10	Oct. 9	Oct. 15	Oct. 13	Oct. 12
Proper 24	Oct 17	Oct. 16	Oct. 22	Oct. 20	Oct. 19
Proper 25	Oct. 24	Oct. 23	Oct. 29	Oct. 27	Oct. 26
Proper 26	Oct. 31	Oct. 30	Nov. 5	Nov. 3	Nov. 2
Proper 27	Nov. 7	Nov. 6	Nov. 12	Nov. 10	Nov. 9
Proper 28	Nov. 14	Nov. 13	Nov. 19	Nov. 17	Nov. 16
Proper 29 (Christ the King)	Nov. 21	Nov. 20	Nov. 26	Nov. 24	Nov. 23

	1998 C	1999 A	2000 B	2001 C
Proper 17	Aug. 30	Aug. 29	Sept. 3	Sept. 2
Proper 18	Sept. 6	Sept. 5	Sept. 10	Sept. 9
Proper 19	Sept. 13	Sept. 12	Sept. 17	Sept. 16
Proper 20	Sept. 20	Sept. 19	Sept. 24	Sept. 23
Proper 21	Sept. 27	Sept. 26	Oct. 1	Sept. 30
Proper 22	Oct. 4	Oct. 3	Oct. 8	Oct. 7
Proper 23	Oct. 11	Oct. 10	Oct. 15	Oct. 14
Proper 24	Oct. 18	Oct. 17	Oct. 22	Oct. 21
Proper 25	Oct. 25	Oct. 24	Oct. 29	Oct. 28
Proper 26	Nov. 1	Oct. 31	Nov. 5	Nov. 4
Proper 27	Nov. 8	Nov. 7	Nov. 12	Nov. 11
Proper 28	Nov. 15	Nov. 14	Nov. 19	Nov. 18
Proper 29 (Christ the King)	Nov. 22	Nov. 21	Nov. 26	Nov. 25